Developmental Disabilities and Sacramental Access

New Paradigms for Sacramental Encounters

Herbert Anderson
Dianne Bergant, C.S.A.
Edward Foley, Capuchin
Mark Francis, C.S.V.
Mary Therese Harrington, S.H.
John Huels, O.S.M.
Barbara Reid, O.P.
Paul Wadell, C.P.

Edward Foley, Capuchin
Editor

A Liturgical Press Book

THE LITURGICAL PRESS
Collegeville, Minnesota

Grateful acknowledgement is given to:

The Catholic Bishops' Conference of England and Wales for permission to reprint *All People Together*, copyright © 1981 by the Catholic Bishops' Conference of England and Wales. All rights reserved.

Archdiocese of Chicago and Liturgy Training Publications for permission to reprint *Access to the Sacraments of Initiation and Reconciliation for Developmentally Disabled Persons*, copyright © 1985, Archdiocese of Chicago. All rights reserved. Liturgy Training Publications, 1800 N. Hermitage Ave., Chicago, IL 60622-1101.

Cover design by Greg Becker

1	2	3	4	5	6	7	8	9

Library of Congress Cataloging-in-Publication Data

Developmental disabilities and sacramental access : new paradigms
   for sacramental encounters / Edward Foley . . . [et al.] ; Edward
   Foley, editor.
      p.   cm.
   Includes bibliographical references.
   ISBN 0-8146-2280-1
   1. Church work with the developmentally disabled—Catholic
Church.   2. Developmentally disabled—Religious life.
3. Sacraments—Catholic Church.   4. Catholic Church—Liturgy.
I. Foley, Edward.
BX2347.8.M4D48   1994
261.8'323—dc20   93-40562
                                                                       CIP

Contents

JUST IN TIME

At age twenty-one, it was becoming more and more difficult for Mark's parents to manage his unpredictable behavior. He was developmentally disabled because of Down Syndrome. Mark had been refused first Communion by several parishes before his parents discovered a special program to prepare adults with developmental disabilities for their first Communion. Since the pastor did not know Mark well, he left it up to Mark's mother to decide which scheduled Eucharist for this special program would be the right time. Mark was so excited when the service began that he hopped down the aisle to his place in the second pew. The pastor had arranged with his mother that she would give Mark the host in order to diminish his anxiety. After he had received, Mark bounced the length of the aisle again. He continued to be very excited at the party that followed the liturgy. On Monday evening, the day after his first Communion, Mark died suddenly and unexpectedly in his sleep.

Introduction

Edward Foley, Capuchin

It is appropriate to begin this volume with a story, since it was a true story that provided the genesis for this project. That story was told to me by Mary Therese Harrington, a staff member of the Special Religious Education Division (SPRED) of the Archdiocese of Chicago, and a contributor to this volume. In the process of discussing another writing project (Harrington 1991) about people with mental retardation, Mary Therese noted the diffculties such people often experience with sacraments in the Roman Catholic Church. When asked to elaborate, she explained that people with mental retardation or other developmental disabilities[1] frequently are refused access to sacraments in the Roman Catholic Church, usually because they have not reached the "age of reason." SPRED staff members constantly hear stories about people with mental disabilities who are not allowed to participate in the sacraments. To emphasize this point, Mary Therese noted that the Chicago SPRED staff had never succeeded in helping people with developmental disabilities enter a sacramental marriage in the Roman Catholic Church.

I was stunned by this revelation and Mary Therese's apparent calm when she spoke of it. When I asked whether she had brought this to the attention of any diocesan or national agencies in the Church, she nodded. In 1979 the National Apostolate with Mentally Retarded Persons (NAMRP)[2] passed the following resolution at its yearly meeting: ''[It is recommended that the] NAMRP provide national leadership to work toward obtaining an official statement of approval for handicapped persons, regardless of the nature or severity of their disabilities, to celebrate the Sacraments of Christian Initiation as full, participating members of God's Church.'' In November 1980 the United States Catholic Conference (USCC) agreed to develop a project that would lead to such a recommendation that could be endorsed by U.S. Roman Catholic bishops. That project was to be achieved through the USCC Advisory Committee on Ministry with Handicapped Individuals. As part of the process approved for the project, Mary Therese and her colleagues began to gather case histories, mostly concerning sacraments of initiation and reconciliation. Many of these were stories about children, young adults, and adults with developmental disabilities who were refused access to sacraments in the Roman Catholic Church. There were also stories about parents or legal guardians who themselves decided that their family members with developmental disabilities did not need the sacraments. Then there were accounts of institutional neglect, where the sacramental needs or desires of people with developmental disabilities were overlooked or ignored in group homes or public institutions.

The inevitable frustration of this venture was tempered by many uplifting accounts of pastors who enthusiastically welcomed those with developmental disabilities, and reports of religious educators who worked tirelessly for their involvement in the faith life of the community. There were also wonderful stories of parents and guardians who were relentless in their struggle to include their loved ones in the full sacramental life of the Church.

This dossier of stories, however, never came to fruition in the hoped-for statement on sacramental participation from the U.S. bishops. Many at the USCC did not perceive that there was any difficulty with current practice. A common reponse was, ''What problem?'' The USCC document was never written. Eventually a document was developed for the Archdiocese of Chicago,[3] which has been adopted by numerous other dioceses.

The stories collected by the SPRED staff, as well as their experiences in preparing and inviting believers with developmental disabilities into the sacramental life of the Church, needed to be told. Yet, simply writing a book—no matter how noble the subject—seemed insufficient, especially in view of the many yet unanswered questions that confront those who struggle with the issue of sacramental access. After some discussion, we decided to gather people from various pastoral and theological disciplines to listen to the SPRED staff tell the stories, to reflect with them upon the significance of these stories for the wider Christian community, and, if appropriate, to gather our reflections for publication.

Six of my colleagues at Catholic Theological Union graciously accepted this invitation: Herbert Anderson, Dianne Bergant, Mark Francis, John Huels, Barbara Reid, and Paul Wadell. Together we embarked upon a series of roundtable discussions and theological reflection with Mary Therese and two of her colleagues from SPRED: James McCarthy, a priest from the Archdiocese of Chicago and founding director of SPRED, and Susanne Gallegher, S.P., an associate director of SPRED. With the support of a grant from Catholic Theological Union, we began a two-year process of listening, reflecting, and writing together.

In the midst of drafting the various sections of the present volume, a notable shift in perspective developed within the group. This process was triggered by Dianne Bergant's introduction of the language of "anomaly" and "normalcy" into our discussions. Dianne's concern was to discover how an Old Testament scholar might contribute to an understanding of the role of people with developmental disabilities in the community of faith when the Old Testament has many passages that quite clearly interpret mental or physical impairment as punishment for wrongdoing. The vehicle for her breakthrough was the language of anomaly.

Dianne pointed out that ancient Israel, like other societies, tended to classify reality—and the people within that reality—in terms of acceptability or unacceptability, purity or pollution, normalcy or anomaly. Although the Priestly tradition of the Old Testament held that people with mental or physical deviations were unacceptable—and, for example, could be excluded from the sacred rituals—the experience of the Exile and the call for incorporation guaranteed by the covenant challenged the prevailing view, and called for a reexamination of the religious status of all people. Traditional standards of normalcy, therefore, gave way to new standards of personal integrity and loyalty to the covenant. This is what Dianne calls a "redefinition of the criteria for access" to the holy in the Old Testament (p. 24).

This explanation of Israel's reinterpretation of itself and its criteria for participation in liturgical celebration found resonance and further development in Paul Wadell's enlightening approach to the issue of sacramentality. Early on, Paul cautioned that our treatment of the issue of sacramental access could itself be discriminatory: giving the impression that those with developmental disabilities would be allowed to participate in the sacraments only because of some exceptional act of charity or extraordinary argument from justice. Such an approach implicitly asserts that those with developmental disabilities are, in fact, marginal to the Christian community. Paul argued, however, that people with developmental disabilities are paradigmatic for the Church's understanding of sacraments and are, in fact, indispensable for an appropriate understanding of the God revealed through Jesus Christ. Thus he concludes that those with developmental disabilities are really "sacraments of God's life and it is we, the allegedly able-bodied, who must first have access to them" (p. 54).

Dianne and Paul's insights offered the project a new and important direction. Thereafter our discussions focused on how people with developmental disabilities are essential to a Christian understanding of ourselves, the liturgy, and the God revealed in Jesus Christ. Recalling Arthur McGill's seminal work *Death and Life* (McGill 1987), the group began to explore how people with developmental disabilities are an essential counterpoint to what McGill calls the "bronze dream," the pervasive conviction in modern U.S. society that we are entitled to live without negatives (p. 25). Sustaining the dream requires an "ethic of avoidance," which creates around us a life apparently without failure. Critical to this ethic is the conviction that death—the ultimate evil—is really outside ordinary human experience, only intrudes by accident, and is the unthinkable enemy (p. 18).

People with developmental disabilities announce exactly what the people of the bronze dream wish to deny: that life is finite, that death embraces us, and that to know God or another human being is to stand in need. In so doing, they announce something essential about being Christian and about living in continuity with Jesus Christ. Therefore, people with developmental disabilities should not simply be allowed to "receive the sacraments" because of the largesse of a particular Christian community. Rather, they need to be raised up in our midst and honored as spiritual guides and friends. They help us to recognize again that sacramental encounters begin with God's graciousness, not with human capacities; that sacramental encounters rely upon the interdependence and openness of a community, not simply upon individual presence; and that sacramental encounters are possible only when each believer admits her or his own inadequacies and disabilities.

Such is the story of the first sacrament, Jesus. Unlike the people of the bronze dream, Jesus lived a life essentially related to death. He chose to die; dying was the very focus and center of his existence (McGill 1987, 46). Jesus proclaimed that choosing to die—refusing to be in total control of one's identity and embracing the finitude of human life—is the only and essential step toward being in God.

Barbara Reid helps us to understand the invitation offered by Jesus to those who would be his disciples. It is an invitation that relies upon God's initiation and does not presume any particular theological skills or training. Rather, it is a free gift that requires only a willingness to believe and follow to the best of one's ability. Jesus is remembered as one who took the initiative with those who were shunned by the community because of their physical or mental state. Ultimately, he identified with every kind of imperfection and brokenness, and announced that only by embracing our inadequacies and brokenness could we enter the kingdom of God. The body of Christ itself is one that is broken and rejected. Genuine encounter with the Holy, as exemplified in the living and dying of Jesus, is only possible when every member of the body—each with his or her own disabilities—is included and embraced.

Such an understanding of Jesus and the whole body of Christ invites a reexamination of our understanding of sacraments. Mark Francis enables such a reexamination by contrasting what he calls a "manualist-scholastic" sacramental model (p. 74), prevalent before the Second Vatican Council, and a post-conciliar sacramental model. The former tends to consider sacraments in isolation from their context, almost treating them as scientific objects to be examined (p. 77). Reliance upon this model led medieval theologians to establish minimum requirements for celebrating a sacrament (p. 79), from both a material and a cognitive perspective. The insistence upon the need for a conceptual understanding of a sacrament before its reception led to the establishment of an "age of reason," before which post-baptismal sacraments were not allowed. In contrast, a post-conciliar approach to sacraments asserts that sacraments cannot be understood apart from the way they are experienced. This means respecting sacraments as symbolic acts. An effective sacramental encounter, therefore, rests upon what Mark calls "symbolic competency," and not upon some predetermined level of cognitive ability.

Reasserting the experiential and symbolic nature of sacraments suggests a decidedly different understanding not only about *who* should be invited into sacraments, but also about *how* one should be invited. Mary Therese makes this point by underscoring how affectivity and symbolic awareness are crucial to effective sacramental catechesis. Faith education is not the same as transmission of knowledge; rather, it is a "call to relate" (p. 117). Establishing a relationship with someone is more a symbolic than a cognitive act. Consequently, sacramental encounters are more affective and symbolic than cognitive. This is especially apparent for those with developmental disabilities. If a person lacks the ability for deductive or inductive reasoning (mental age about twelve to fourteen), trying to explain the content of faith to them will do little good. Even if one has these abilities, propositional forms of catechesis are insufficient. Again, those with developmental disabilities not only indicate their own need for affective and symbolic catechesis, but illuminate the essential nature of this kind of sacramental catechesis for all.

These approaches to sacrament and sacramental catechesis are not new. They are traditional in the fullest sense of the term, and find great support in the law of the Church. John Huels demonstrates as much in his treatment of the rights of persons with developmental disabilities regarding the sacraments of baptism, confirmation, Eucharist, penance, and anointing of the sick. According to Roman Catholic law, all the baptized have a right to the sacraments, a right that can be restricted only if there are clear legal grounds. John asserts that "there are no clear legal grounds for denying Catholics with developmental disabilities access to the liturgical rites in question" (pp. 95). This canonical assessment is based on the theological premise noted above: sacraments begin with God's graciousness. This graciousness is revealed in baptism, in which the Christian community proclaims the radical equality of all God's children.

While there is a good deal of consensus among the authors, and numerous common threads, this volume does not signal the end of the debate nor resolution on the issue of the role of people with developmental disabilities in the sacramental life of the Church. While acknowledging this role as paradigmatic, we also admit that it poses many unresolved problems. Our inability even to begin addressing the question of sacramental marriage for those with developmental disabilities is glaring evidence of that.

The ambiguity of much of this area is demonstrated by real stories that punctuate this volume. Although names and places have been altered to respect the identity of the participants, the stories are true. Some of them are uplifting, positive episodes; some are astonishingly distressing. Both are part of the reality of the Roman Catholic Church today. They are incorporated here not primarily to illustrate the various contributions of the authors, but to summon in concrete the real issues and real people that prompted us to engage in this project in the first place.

Finally, as Herbert Anderson poignantly notes in the Epilogue, issues of sacramental access are only one small part of the mystery, joy, and struggle of individuals and families faced with developmental disabilities. Sometimes the experience leads to deeper faith and stronger family ties. Other times, however, such disabilities are a source of anguish, shame, and grief. Faith is tested, relationships are strained, and hope is all but extinguished. There is no illusion here that our reinterpretation of biblical faith, suggestions for new catechesis, or analysis of canon law can remove this pain or restore waning faith. It is our sincere hope, however, that this volume may, in some small measure, symbolize our care for the people behind the issues and our heartfelt empathy for those who struggle with developmental disabilities. And it is to those who so struggle that we reverently dedicate this volume.

NOTES

1. A developmental disability originates before age eighteen, continues indefinitely and constitutes a substantial handicap. It is not a mental illness or other type of illness, but a developmental condition. Developmental disabilities include mental retardation, epilepsy, cerebral palsy, and autism.

2. This organization is currently reconsidering its name, and may change it in the near future.

3. *Access to the Sacraments of Initiation and Reconciliation for Developmentally Disabled Persons: Pastoral Guidelines for the Archdiocese of Chicago* (1985), published in the appendix of this volume.

REFERENCES

Harrington, Mary Therese. *A Place for All: Mental Retardation, Catechesis and Liturgy.* American Essays in Liturgy. Collegeville: The Liturgical Press, 1991.

McGill, Arthur. *Death and Life.* Eds. Charles A. Wilson and Per M. Anderson. Philadelphia: Fortress Press, 1987.

1

"Come, let us go up to the mountain of the Lord" (Isa 2:3)

Biblical Reflections on the Question of Sacramental Access

Dianne Bergant, C.S.A.

> "Marginal life" is an expression frequently applied to various groups of people who do not fit into classifications such as "normal" or "mainstream." (Dougherty 1984, 12).

Thus does the first director of STAUROS[1] enable us to understand better that the people who belong to the groups he mentions (those with developmental disadvantage) usually are forced into marginality by circumstances and powers beyond their control. Someone other than themselves has either deprived them of the means that are necessary for full and satisfying living and, thereby, driven them to the margins of society, or has furnished for them a tragically unjust judgement regarding their human potential and the quality of their lives. Too frequently their situations have rendered them powerless to oppose this marginalization; in fact, their inability to offer resistance has only reinforced their own vulnerability.

It is not uncommon for people to take for granted their standing in society, a standing which is usually the outgrowth of their uncritical acceptance of the dominant social attitudes regarding gender, racial, economic, or physical factors. We are all born finite beings with numerous limitations and various degrees of disability, but the institutions of our society presuppose or demand a certain standardized style of living. Those who are able to meet these standards, and are thereby judged to be normal, perpetuate the power of the standardizing institutions by their conformity; those who cannot comply to the standards often are denied access to the resources of life that the society offers and are relegated to its margins. Even people who are sensitive to such situations too often are inclined to accept them as inevitable and to assume that there is nothing that can be done to change them. These people may instinctively recoil at what they perceive to be injustice, but at the same time they might be supporting the very dynamics that create such situations. These dynamics are usually embedded in the prevailing culture and are unconsciously accepted. For this reason, a cursory examination of some societal expectations may help to put into context the following biblical reflections relating to the matter of sacramental access for people who have developmental disabilities.

It is important to admit at the outset that turning to the Bible for guidance can itself create problems. There are many passages that quite clearly interpret suffering as punishment for wrongdoing. We read, "And the LORD will strike you with madness, blindness and panic, so that even at midday you will grope like a blind man in the dark, unable to find your way" (Deut 28:28-29). This attitude toward disability is not limited to the religious tradition of ancient Israel. It seems that during the time of Jesus, sick people were thought to be ruled by demons that resided within them. "Jesus rebuked him and the devil came out of him, and from that hour the boy was cured" (Matt 17:18). Contemporary sensitivities may cringe in the face of such attitudes, but how are we to understand the biblical teaching that appears to support them?

This article is an attempt at such understanding. It will not try to justify the ancient biblical beliefs and judgements but to understand them as Israel intended that they be understood. It will begin with a brief look at the natural human tendency to classify reality and an example of this tendency taken from the biblical account of creation. This will be followed by an explanation of the nature of ritual and the interrelationship between sacred space, time, and status. Then there will be a description of the shift that took place in ancient Israel's perception of sacred status and the revision of the criteria for crossing sacred boundaries that this shift produced. Next, the concepts of purity and pollution will be examined in order to understand how they functioned as criteria for crossing sacred boundaries. This will be followed by a description of the shift from restrictive standards of cultic purity to more encompassing demands of covenant fidelity in determining religious acceptability.

"Everything according to its kind" (Gen 1:11-12, 20, 24-25)

Extensive research has led anthropologists to conclude that human beings have an inherent need to clarify and to separate or classify aspects of reality into categories so that meaning can be ascribed to them and suitable behaviors assigned. Their studies have also provided us with evidence that the particular meaning given to reality may be largely determined by a social group and not be universally held. Thus different groups may have the same or similarly designed organizations or customs, yet these may carry very dissimilar meanings. (For example, driving on the left side of the road *is* sometimes right.) Cultures develop systems of beliefs within which particular realities are arranged and made comprehensible, and they attach symbols or names to these realities. In other words, we organize reality into categories in order to understand it and to exercise some manner of control over it.

Turning to the Bible, we see that the separation of created beings and their classification into recognizable categories is a prominent theme in the Priestly tradition of the Pentateuch. The first of the two creation narratives in the Book of Genesis (1:1–2:4a) depicts God separating the light from darkness and naming them "day" and "night" respectively (1:4-5), and then separating the waters above the firmament from the waters below and naming the firmament "the heavens" (1:6-7). Next, living things are made with the ability to reproduce "according to [their] kind" (vv. 1:11-12, 20, 24-25). This power of reproduction is another indication of the order inherent in the

LIVING AS FRIENDS WHO FORGIVE

The practice of reconciliation for a group of young people be-
tween the ages of fourteen amd sixteen who are in an institu-
tional setting occurs within their daily life experience. After a
brief Liturgy of the Word, each person is invited to pray in si-
lence to Jesus for what they have done wrong. If they want to
receive the pardon of God, they are to put their hands into the
hands of the priest and say ''Yes, Amen.'' When this is com-
pleted, they hold hands to show that they want to love one an-
other and live as friends. The ceremony concludes with singing
the Our Father while they continue to hold hands. Almost al-
ways, at the end of this liturgy for reconciliation, the young
people sing a song they like several times. This liturgy does not
work well when the parents are present.

very structures of nature, and the phrase "according to their kind" denotes the human instinct to classify.

At the end of each day of creation, the separation and classification or naming that took place that day are scrutinized, and the order established is declared "good" (vv. 4, 10, 12, 18, 21, 25, 31). The crowning action of creation is God's blessing (or "setting apart") and making holy the seventh day (2:3). The Sabbath, or divine rest, is a sign of the completion of God's creative ordering. It is a sign that the order established by the creator God is permanent and will not be disturbed by another creative act. The consecration of the Sabbath signifies that the natural order of time has religious meaning. The liturgical character of the week is an indication of Israel's conviction that at the heart of this created order is a fundamental ritual order.

For the Priestly writers, creation and ritual cannot be separated. They believed that in liturgical celebration three different orders come together as one: the order within natural creation, the order of society, and ritual order. The importance of this convergence cannot be overemphasized. In general, ritual can be understood in several different ways. It can refer to social behavior that is either ordinary (profane) or extraordinary (sacred). As used in this context, ritual refers to a complex performance of symbolic acts that control the activities, patterns, and relationships within society. It tells us what to do (activities), how this should be done (patterns), and by whom (relationships).

Ritual achieves its control in these areas in various ways. It grants religious authority to the social order, and it reinforces this authority each time the ritual is reenacted. For example, in ancient Israel the ceremony of the coronation of the king was itself considered the act of divine adoption (Ps 110). The ritual of coronation or divine adoption was an assurance that the rule of the king was divinely decreed. Furthermore, whenever the people recited psalms that praise God for establishing the Davidic dynasty at the time of the foundation of the world (Ps 89), they reinforced the notion that this dynasty was part of the very order of creation.

Ritual also provides a way of restoring social order when we judge that it has been disturbed or upset by some kind of confusion of categories. This reestablishment of order is accomplished by means of rites of passage (ceremonies that dramatize movement from one stage to another). For example, Israel believed that mysterious and dangerous life powers were released at the time of childbirth, and so a woman had to undergo a rite of purification after forty days if the child was male and after eighty days if it was female (Lev 12:1-5).

Ritual is also concerned with specific dimensions of space, time, and status or the sacred standing of the participants (Gorman 1990). First, sacred space is that point where the divine and the human worlds converge. It is a holy place and, therefore, it is also a dangerous place. For this reason it must be marked by boundaries and thresholds which only sacred people can cross. The wilderness tabernacle and later the Jerusalem Temple were Israel's sacred spaces par excellence, and the Bible contains many rules that governed entrance into these sacred precincts.

Second, ritual involves sacred time. While time itself can be understood as linear (non-recurring) or as cyclic (recurring), sacred time is the human reproduction of primeval or cosmogonic time (*illo tempore*, ''in that time''). It is marked by rituals and ceremonies that protect people as they pass from one kind of time to another. It is through ritual that sacred time is repeatable and the power of the world of the holy permeates the world of the profane. In Israel, certain events of historical time became sacred time. The most significant of these was the deliverance from Egypt. Every ritual commemoration of this event made its sacredness present to the community. Therefore, Israel's ceremonies were both reenactments of primeval time (creation) and remembrances of momentous historical events (deliverance).

Third, ritual involves sacred status or the standing of the ritual participants. Status can be understood in terms of institutional roles or categories of purity and pollution (Gorman 1990, 10). A preeminent institutional role was that of the priest, whose responsibility it was to safeguard sacred space and time and to act as a bridge for those who had to cross from the profane to the sacred and back again. The concepts of purity and pollution are related to sacred status and do not belong so much to the realm of morality as to that of normality. They pertain to the conformity or lack of conformity to the norms or categories that defined the order of things.

In a well-ordered society, sacred space, time, and status are usually interrelated. However, at a time of social disorganization, their relationship is often significantly altered. The present study, with its focus on access to the sacred, will show that a shift in the perception of sacred status took place in ancient Israel. This shift called for a revision of the criteria for crossing sacred boundaries. In order to understand sacred status, however, it will be important first to be clear about what purity and pollution imply.

"Distinguish between what is clean and what is unclean" (Lev 10:10)

Sometimes events or situations do not fit completely within the categories set by the group, and thus appear to be out of order. These exceptions to the rule are called anomalies and they can range from the presence of dirt (understood as matter out of place), to an eclipse of the sun or the moon, to multiple births, to a developmental impairment. The initial response to an anomaly may be either curiosity or anxiety or both. Curiosity frequently is a prelude to ridicule; anxiety usually leads to suppression or avoidance. Some anomalous situations fascinate us as long as they are restrained or kept at a distance.

Societies have long designed ways of understanding and handling those situations that are in some way anomalous. One such way has been through rules overseeing purity. These laws, concerned with bodily orifices and fluids, were intended to ensure that only what conformed to the norm could approach God or people, places, and things dedicated to God. These purity laws governed ritual and, by extension, social behavior. Since the human body is regarded as a microcosm of the entire world (the macrocosm), body consciousness often reflects social consciousness. Our attitudes toward social groups and behavior are revealed in the manner in which we react to our bodies. A proliferation of purification rules, as is found in the Pentateuch, indicates an undeniable concern for social order and for the anomalies, especially human, physical ones, that defy that order.

Purification rules can deal with an anomaly in several different ways. They might either separate it from the rest of the group (only what is without blemish can be sacrificed to God, Lev 22:19), or integrate it into the group once it has been brought into conformity with the order determined by the group (someone cured of leprosy is brought back into the community, Lev 14:9). The rules can also help the group to negotiate a modification of its categories and, thereby, completely change its classification of reality. This kind of change might radically redefine what had previously been considered an anomaly. The present article will attempt to show that, besides reinforcing social discrimination by including only those people and objects that conform to the norm, the language of ritual can be modified to create a new world order where human events and situations take on significantly new and different meaning. When this happens, what was once excluded from the circle of acceptability can be embraced.

Israel's purification rituals (Lev 11–16) served as rites of passage, reinstating people, things, and places previously considered unclean or unfit for worship. (Cleanness or purity denoted conformity to a material pattern, not to a moral standard.) But we must ask, do the rites of passage only operate after what formerly had been an exception has conformed to the rule, or might the rites themselves incorporate the individual without demanding conformity? If the latter is the case, the rites of passage would themselves be a way of redefining the character of the group. We will see that this is precisely what happened in ancient Israel.

All the laws regulating purity hinge on the concept of order within creation. Animals were classified according to their natural habitat (waters, heavens, and dry land), and their customary manner of movement (swimming, flying, crawling, and creeping). Whatever did not conform to these norms was considered unclean and was to be avoided (Douglas 1966, 100–116). Avoidance of this kind of irregularity may have ensured a concept of right order and cultic purity, but when conformity to categories was imposed upon the human community it also engendered discrimination against those who for any reason at all did not meet the specifications of the norm. Furthermore, it reinforced the cultural, racial, gender, and developmental biases of those within the society who had the authority to determine the norms. In many situations today, it continues to discriminate against people. Separation, which is helpful in identifying what belongs to the group, can also be harmful because it either excludes or marginalizes what does not conform to a very specific standard.

People who do not fit into the classifications are frequently forced to live marginal lives. When social institutions and structures are established according to patterns of normalcy, the inability of some people to conform prevents them from participating fully in the organizations or activities of the group. Too often they are regarded as less than human, their movement is restricted, their existence is circumscribed, and they are denied access to much that society offers for a fulfilling life. This certainly is true today despite the fact that the classifications that are prominent in contemporary society seldom have anything to do with cultic purity.

Despite its concern for purity, ancient Israel still found some of its purification laws problematic. Especially at the time of the Exile, the people were caught in a dramatic struggle between the marginalization dictated by standards of cultic purity and the incorporation guaranteed by covenant affiliation. New criteria for determining religious acceptability emerged out of this struggle.

"An Eternal Covenant" (Gen 9:16; 17:7; Exod 31:16)

The Priestly tradition divides the early history of Israel into four periods, associated with Adam, Noah, Abraham, and Moses. Although the periods of Adam and Noah differ in narrative sequence, they both belong to primeval time and in this study will be considered the primeval period.[2] The Priestly tradition marks each of these periods by a covenant initiated by God, thus indicating the sacredness of this early history. The covenants are made with Noah (Gen 9), Abraham (Gen 17), and Moses (Exod 31).[3] This narrative scheme is not merely a division into neat linear blocks; it is a pattern that gradually brings the ritual bias of the Priestly tradition into clear focus.

The first covenant is made with the entire created order; the second narrows the divine/human relationship to one family among many; the third concentrates on what is considered the most important aspect of the life of that family, namely, ritual. These covenants all exhibit distinct Priestly characteristics: (1) Each brings to completion an aspect of the initial drama of creation as found in the Genesis 1 account. (2) Each is related to one of the orders described above (cosmic, social, cultic). (3) Each is given meaning and force by the addition of a promise and a sign, the nature of which identifies the character of the respective covenant. (4) Although it is made with one person, each extends to everything included in the particular order to which it is related (all of creation, all of the descendants of Abraham, the entire cultic community).

Covenant with Noah. In one of the first acts of creation, God fixed the firmament as the safeguard of cosmic order, confining the chaotic waters in their appointed place (Gen 1:6-7). This order is established again after the waters are allowed to encompass the earth in the devastating flood. God promises that this newly established cosmic order will be eternal and this promise is confirmed with a cosmic sign that stretches across the firmament, the bow in the sky (Gen 9:1-17). Though negotiated with Noah, the covenant extends to all of natural creation.

Covenant with Abraham. The original relationship between God and humankind was characterized in the creation narrative by the expression ''image of God'' (Gen 1:26-28). A new relationship is established with Abraham and his descendants. This covenant involves a promise of abundant posterity, as well as eternal duration. Circumcision, the sign of this covenant, is a mark in human flesh. It establishes a social order in which Abraham and all of his descendants are regarded as separate from all other people (Gen 17:1-14).

Covenant with Moses. At the time of creation, God set one day apart from all other days as a period of sanctified rest (Gen 2:1-3). At Sinai, a complete cultic ordering of time, as well as persons and objects, is decreed. Sabbath, the sign of this third covenant, becomes the eternal remembrance of God's role as creator and sanctifier. Observance of the Sabbath connects the entire people with the order of creation.

This examination of the covenant tradition shows that not only did the Priestly writers arrange history according to this gradual narrowing of focus (cosmic to social to cultic), but these three spheres are reflected in the fundamental components of the ritual tradition, namely, sacred space, sacred time, and sacred status. The tabernacle, which was regarded as the counterpart of cosmic order created during primeval time, marked the location of sacred space; the calendar of festivals and liturgical remembrances, which complemented the celebration of the Sabbath, ordered sacred time; and the purification rites, which certified social acceptance, determined sacred status. The underlying conviction of the Priestly tradition was belief in the holiness of God, with the accompanying charge of holiness on the part of the people. The major aspects of divine holiness—wealth of power, absolute unapproachability, vitality, transcendence, and fascination (Otto 1928)—required that only what was clean (i.e., intact and in its proper class) was considered fit to approach the holy. Thus cleanness or cultic purity was the proper human counterpart of God's holiness.

This religious system of purity was challenged at the time of the Exile, when the Temple had been destroyed and the people scattered, some transported to Babylon while others were left behind to rebuild their social and religious lives. Those who remained in the land of Israel may have been able to assemble in or near the ruins of the Temple to pray and pay homage to their God, but the exiles certainly did not have the freedom to construct a shrine in Babylon. Without the Temple and its elaborate layout of sacred precincts, the people had to reexamine their notions of sacred space. Even more basic to this dilemma was the question of the likelihood of God's presence in a foreign land. Babylon was dedicated to other gods. Would the God of Israel accompany the people in their deportation and continue to be with them throughout their Exile? And if God would remain with them, how would they understand God's presence in their midst and symbolize it? Even more troubling was the claim of the prophet Ezekiel, that before any of this happened, the glory of God left the Temple and, therefore, the midst of the people (Ezek 11:23).

Without a specific physical site to identify as the place of God's presence, other elements of cultic purity had to be reexamined. Since the people could still assign religious significance to certain days and seasons, sacred time took on new meaning and the liturgical calendar took on new importance. The manner in which they would commemorate these times might have to be radically changed, since they had no Temple within which to celebrate, but significant times could still be set aside as religious memorials. In fact, many commentators maintain that it was at this time that the Sabbath attained the significance that it has come to enjoy.

Finally, residing in a foreign land and being deprived of the sacred shrine required a new way of understanding religious purity, or sacred status, and how the lives of people were to be regulated by it. Priests had no sacred space to safeguard or to guide into and out of by means of rites of passage. Therefore, their role and importance changed. Even more importantly, the entire land of Babylon, wherein the Israelites lived, was unclean according to their laws of purity. This meant that the religious status of *all* of the people had to be determined in a new way. Traditional standards of normalcy could no longer be invoked to make this determination. It was most likely at this time that personal integrity and loyalty to the covenant, which were always important elements in the religion of Israel (see Mic 6:8), took on heightened meaning. These became the criteria for determining the religious purity necessary for entrance into the presence of God. Conformity to these standards flowed from a decision freely made by the individual rather than from a fixed pattern imposed by the group. Thus the meaningful yet restrictive standards of cultic purity gave way to the more encompassing demands of covenant fidelity. This redefinition of the criteria for access is clearly stated in several psalms, two of which will be examined here.

"Who may stand in the holy place?" (Ps 24:3)

Psalms 15 and 24 are quite clear in their insistence on interior rather than ritual purity as a requirement for entrance to the holy place. It may very well be that such psalms were sung in the Temple before its destruction, but the Exile provoked such a refocusing of the theological point of view that a particular theology which may not have been central at one time became so at another.

Psalm 15 falls easily into three parts: a request for information about requirements for entrance into the holy place (v. 1), a response in the form of "Torah instruction" (vv. 2-5a), and a promise of blessing as reward for compliance to the Torah teaching (v. 5b). The first part clearly asks about matters related to cultic purity. Who is clean enough to approach God? "Tent" and "holy mountain" are both references to sacred place, perhaps initially to Mount Zion, the site of the Temple. The purification regulations found in Leviticus would respond to this request with a list of standards for external conformity. However, the psalm does not provide such a response. Instead, it sets forth norms for righteous living along the lines found in the prophetic tradition. Although this set of norms is not a comprehensive one, its list of ten ways in which righteous believers demonstrate eligibility for entrance to the presence of God is reminiscent of the "ten words" of the Decalogue. The psalm contains an orderly arrangement of the actions the righteous do and those they refrain from doing. They walk blamelessly, do justice, and think truth; they do not slander, harm, or reproach. They despise the reprobate and honor the God-fearer; they do not change their word nor lend money at usury.

Such a style of living is reminiscent of the "way of the wise" as found in so many places in the Book of Proverbs, a section of the Bible apparently unconcerned with ritual practice. This psalm suggests that access to the holy place is achieved through a life of fundamental moral integrity. For an Israelite, this life was certainly in accord with the instructions laid down in the Torah or Law, but it was still a life of basic social virtue that could be practiced by anyone and certainly not one simply of ritual conformity to specific Israelite requirements.

Psalm 24 contains theology that is quite similar to that found in Psalm 15. It too can be divided into three parts: an acknowledgement of God's rule over all creation (vv. 1-2), structure and content identical to that of Psalm 15 (vv. 3-6), and lyrics sung during a liturgical procession (vv. 7-10). The psalm is an example of the liturgical celebration of the historicization of the victory of the creator God over cosmic enemies. The account of this battle between the forces of two gods follows a mythical pattern that was very common in the ancient Near Eastern world. According to the myth, one of the gods was the embodiment of order and the other was a comparable embodiment of chaos. Chaos was conquered and its forces were checked. The victorious warrior god restored the cosmic order that had been threatened, entered triumphantly into the city, constructed and took up residence in the temple-palace, and in this way established peace. Thus, the first part of this psalm alludes to creation (v. 2) and the third part to the triumphant procession into the Temple (vv. 7-10).

Although the psalm uses creation language, God is also described as "mighty in battle" (v. 8) and is called "YHWH of hosts" (v. 10), references with military implications. The entrance of God (vv. 7-10) might refer to the procession of the ark of the covenant as it was carried into battle (see Num 10:35f.). Thus the psalm praises the triumphant march of the primordial creator and warrior God who enters both the cosmic Temple and the Promised Land. In Israel's liturgical recital, three elements from the creation myth were historicized: the oppressive powers of Egypt and the Canaanite states were portrayed as the concrete embodiment of cosmic chaos; the characteristics of the valiant warrior God were attributed to the God of Israel; and God and the people marched exultantly into the Temple where God would reign supreme. We see in this psalm what was mentioned above, namely, that in Israel certain events of historical time became sacred time.

The psalm not only alludes to the liturgical commemoration of cosmic and historical victory but also describes those who will be admitted into the sacred precincts to celebrate God's victory (v. 3). They are those whose hands are sinless and whose hearts are clean. "Sinless hands" symbolizes upright living and characterizes a way of social interaction that is unselfish and trustworthy. "A clean heart" denotes innocence before God. Psalm 24, like Psalm 15, proclaims that it is moral uprightness, not ritual purity, that qualifies one for access to the holy place, there to pay homage to the holy God.

Even this cursory examination of selected passages from the Bible shows that, while ancient Israel did not relinquish its conviction that only what is holy can approach the Holy, it radically modified its concepts of holiness and the liturgical regulations that flowed from them, once the circumstances of its life had changed. In fact, the purity laws never presumed that human beings would ever be equal to and, therefore, deserving of access to the power and blessedness of God. They were merely attempts to acknowledge the awesomeness of the divine and the human need to remember the extraordinary (sacred) dimension of what is otherwise ordinary (profane).

"Come, let us go up to the mountain of the Lord" (Isa 2:3; Mic 4:2)

What conclusions can be drawn from this study that might address the question of access to the sacraments for those who have some form of developmental impairment? The first conclusion addresses the fundamental question of anthropology, or the way a society understands what it means to be human. Since criteria governing access to the holy are determined by the world view or system of meaning that undergirds a culture, some grasp of this underlying system is indispensable. If, for any reason, this system of meaning is disturbed, the structures and practices of the culture should be reexamined and redefined lest they be retained despite becoming devoid of meaning. Since structures and customs arise in order to express and preserve values that the group cherishes, systems of meaning should also be reexamined in order to reclaim any normative values embedded in outmoded structures and customs, so that these values can be expressed in new and more meaningful ways.

The Exile, with its social and religious upheaval and the collapse of cultic observance, forced Israel into just such a situation of reexamination, redefinition, and new expression. Many scholars believe that, rather than cling to an outmoded past and risk losing its authenticity, Israel chose to reinterpret itself and therefore it emerged from the Exile with a deeper spirituality.

The contemporary world no longer subscribes to an anthropology that limits full humanity to those possessed of specific gender, racial, economic, or physical or mental characteristics. This shift in perspective clearly redefines what might be considered an anomaly. Our social customs and laws do not always reflect a more inclusive anthropology, but the contemporary world does support the rights of the individual, in theory if not in practice. Furthermore, when a flagrant abuse of these rights occurs, steps are usually taken to remedy the abusive situation. Any denial of access to the resources of society to people with impairment is seen today as an abuse.

On the other hand, many religions still maintain structures and practices that designate sacred space, time, and status. At issue is not whether or not they should make such designations but whether or not the criteria used to do so is consistent with the prevailing systems of meaning. If a society no longer reckons full participation according to obsolete standards of normalcy, no group within that society can continue to employ such standards without jeopardizing its credibility or effectiveness. This study has provided one example of how Israel adjusted some of its cultic regulations when the situation within the broader society called for it. Religious bodies today can do no less if they are to be true both to their enduring religious values and to their variable cultural settings.

A second conclusion to be drawn relates more specifically to the change in the criteria for participation in liturgical celebration found in the biblical tradition. The psalms clearly show that covenantal commitment, which expressed itself in both devotion to God (pure heart) and social integrity (clean hands), qualified one for access to the holy place. Furthermore, it was these attributes rather than cultic purity that were preached by the prophets of ancient Israel (Amos 5:22-24) as well as by Christianity (Matt 22:37-40, Mark 12:29-31, Luke 10:27). Love of God and concern for the welfare of others are far more important standards of judgement than are physical health or mental aptitude.

A third conclusion drawn from this study deals with the role that ritual plays in constructing social identity. It not only controls the activities, patterns, and relationships within society, it also creates them. Ritual proclaims and celebrates what has already been accomplished, and it announces and anticipates what has not yet been fully realized. It is itself a sacramental or symbolic act that creates the reality that it signifies. It begins a kind of transformation of society that is meant to spread beyond the confines of the gathered assembly. The participation to which it invites community members during the liturgy is intended to extend to other social settings. Just as the celebration of the coronation of the king established him as the adopted son of God, so baptism actually incorporates the neophyte into the community (Eph 4:4-6) and Eucharistic sharing bonds the communicants to each other (1 Cor 10:16-17). This incorporation and bonding continue after the liturgy has concluded, for a new reality has been created. Therefore, incorporating people into the assembly who previously were excluded redefines the very character of the assembly.

The final conclusion may well be the most challenging one. It is time that we admit that we are all in some ways disabled. The very process of aging involves degrees of physical and mental diminishment. Therefore, if the norms for understanding what it means to be human do not issue from an unreal notion of perfection, what is their origin? A second look at the Priestly tradition shows that, while there is definitely a ritual bias, basic to the entire tradition is the notion of covenant. Moreover, each of the three covenant narratives examined above include two principal features. First, the human partner is never self-possessed or self-reliant. Second, the human partner is always a member of a broader community that is in covenant with God. It would seem that vulnerability and social interdependence are at the heart of what it means to be a human. Yet the very people who exemplify such vulnerability and social interdependence are often the ones forced to the margins of society, there to remain silent and invisible. Not only is this insult to their human dignity a grave miscarriage

RAYMOND MUST CONFESS
BEFORE HE CAN COMMUNE

Raymond is a moderately retarded boy, nine years old. He had been prepared through a special religious education program to make his first Communion with the other children in the parish. When the day arrived, the children assembled in the back of the church for the entrance procession. Just before the service was to begin, the pastor pulled Raymond from the line to ask if he had received first penance. Since he had not, the pastor announced that Raymond would not be allowed to receive his first Communion. After an intense conversation with his mother, the pastor held up the service long enough to take Raymond into another room and hear his confession. Raymond was so frightened by the interruption that he did not speak. As a result, the pastor postponed the first Communion.

of justice, it also enables the rest of society to deny its own limitations and various degrees of disability, its defenselessness and its dependency.

The challenge before the community may not be merely the loving and remorseful inclusion of all who have been unjustly barred from full liturgical participation, as imperative as this may be. The real challenge may be the design of a new model for understanding what it means to be human. Such a model must be based on an acknowledgement of our fundamental human finitude, our lack of absolute control over our lives, and our inherent need of others. It will include rather than segregate people, support rather than burden them, praise the Creator rather than denigrate creation. It will invite all: "Come, let us go up to the mountain of the Lord, to the house of the God of Jacob."

NOTES

1. STAUROS is an international ecumenical organization sponsored by the Congregation of the Passion that conducts studies and projects on various aspects of human suffering. Its offices are in Chicago.

2. "Scholars currently agree that the narrative of the flood and the eventual recession of the waters is a second creation story, coming from the same theological tradition and highlighting much of the same theology as found in Genesis 1. In fact, in the traditions of many early civilizations, the flood narrative was identical with the creation narrative. The destructive flood was really the primeval flood, and the individual saved was the first created human being. This suggests that both creation and flood were viewed as primeval happenings, not as historical events. Israel's flood account contains some of the very vocabulary found in the creation report. The abyss (*t̆hom*) was in place before God separated the waters (Gen 1,2). This same abyss burst open causing the flood (Gen 7,11), and was closed when God decreed its end (8,2). Both narratives mention a wind (*ruaḥ*) that swept over the cosmic abyss (1,1; 8,1). It was God's intent that the animals 'be fertile and multiply' (1,22; 8,17). The same blessing with the commission to rule over the animals is given to humankind in both passages (1,28; 9,1-2)" (Bergant 1990, 11).

3. The following is a summary of the work done by Habel (1971, 65-84). See also Cross (1973, 293-325) and Klein (1979, 125-48).

REFERENCES

Bergant, Dianne. "Is the Biblical Worldview Anthropocentric?" *New Theology Review* 4, no. 2 (1990) 5–14.

Cross, Frank Moore. *Canaanite Myth and Hebrew Epic.* Cambridge: Harvard University Press, 1973.

Dougherty, Flavian, ed. *The Deprived, the Disabled and the Fullness of Life.* Wilmington, Del.: Michael Glazier, 1984.

Douglas, Mary. *Purity and Danger: An Analysis of Concepts of Pollution and Taboo.* London: Routledge & Kegan Paul, 1966.

Gorman, Frank H., Jr. *The Ideology of Ritual: Space, Time and Status in the Priestly Theology.* Journal of the Study of the Old Testament 91. Sheffield: Sheffield Press, 1990.

Habel, Norman. *Literary Criticism of the Old Testament.* Philadelphia: Fortress, 1971.

Klein, Ralph W. *Israel in Exile.* Philadelphia: Fortress, 1979.

Otto, Rudolph. *The Idea of the Holy.* 9th ed. Trans. John W. Harvey. Oxford: Oxford University Press, 1928.

FURTHER READING

Brueggemann, Walter. *Israel's Praise: Doxology Against Idolatry and Ideology.* Philadelphia: Fortress, 1988. An examination of how ritual use of the psalms fashions a new communal reality.

———. *Abiding Astonishment: Psalms, Modernity, and the Making of History.* Louisville: Westminster/John Knox, 1991. A contemporary pastoral interpretation of the psalms.

Dougherty, Flavian, ed. *The Deprived, the Disabled and the Fullness of Life.* Wilmington: Michael Glazier, 1984. A series of essays that address disability and meaningful life.

Douglas, Mary. *Purity and Danger: An Analysis of Concepts of Pollution and Taboo.* London: Routledge & Kegan Paul, 1966. A landmark on purity laws.

2

The Whole Broken Body of Christ

New Testament Reflections on
Access to the Holy through Jesus

Barbara Reid, O.P.

When asking questions about sacramental access for persons with developmental disabilities, it is essential to examine Jesus' attitudes and practices as revealed in the Gospels. There we find that Jesus himself is the sacrament of God—the locus for graced encounters with the holy. In this essay, we will examine several gospel episodes that illustrate how this is so.

In the Gospels of Mark and John, we find stories demonstrating that there are no prerequisites of theological education or understanding for entering a graced encounter with Jesus. It is faith that opens one to Jesus' freely offered self-gift. The desired response is a willingness to follow Jesus, who draws one into deeper knowledge and experience of the holy. This sacramental experience is communal; the faith of the whole body bears up the individual believers, with all their capacities and disabilities.

Most frequently Jesus initiates the interaction, deliberately seeking out those who are marginalized and considered unclean. Even more radical than associating with persons thought to be impure is Jesus' deliberate choice of this identity for himself. By this self-identification he reinterprets the meaning of

God-likeness. The body of Christ is one that is broken and cast out; it is this body through which one gains access to the holy. The Church, then, as the body of Christ, cannot be whole nor mediate the holy unless it fully includes every member, each with their brokenness and their gifts. In light of Jesus' self-identification with people in their brokenness, the question of admitting persons with developmental disabilities to the sacraments appears to be formulated backwards. We might ask, instead, whether sacramental celebrations without the full participation of persons with disabilities are not devoid of their most basic meaning.

Disciples in the Gospel of Mark

The Gospel of Mark, the first Gospel to be written, paints a most uncomplimentary picture of Jesus' first disciples. Part of Mark's purpose is to show the struggle entailed in being a disciple, particularly the struggle to understand Jesus and his message. Theological understanding comes only with the completion of Jesus' passion, death, and resurrection.

The entire first half of Mark's Gospel is permeated with questions. For example, the first cure (1:21-28) takes place in the synagogue in Capernaum where Jesus is teaching. After Jesus exorcises an unclean spirit the witnesses exclaim, "What is this? A new teaching—with authority!"[1] Similarly, after Jesus heals and forgives a man who was paralyzed (2:1-12), bystanders ask, "Why does this fellow speak this way? . . . Who can forgive sins but God alone?" (2:7). Seeing Jesus at dinner with Levi and his tax collector friends, the Pharisees ask, "Why does he eat with tax collectors and sinners?" (2:16). After the stilling of the storm on the Sea of Galilee, Jesus' disciples query, "Who then is this, that even the wind and sea obey him?" (4:41). At home in Nazareth, Jesus' Sabbath teaching in the synagogue evokes the questions, "Where did this man get all this? What is this wisdom that has been given to him? What deeds of power are being done by his hands! Is not this the carpenter . . . ?" (6:1-6). King Herod puzzles over whether Jesus could be John the Baptist raised from the dead, while others postulate Elijah, or a prophet (6:14-16).

The climax to the suspense that Mark has created comes in the famous passage where Jesus asks his disciples, "Who do people say that I am?" (8:27). The reader knows the correct answer from the first verse of the gospel: "Jesus Christ, the Son of God." But none of the characters in the story know, except the demons: "I know who you are, the Holy One of God!" (1:24; also 1:34; 3:11; 5:7). Peter's answer, "You are the Messiah," (8:29) is correct, but he and the other disciples still do not understand its meaning.

The remainder of the Gospel unfolds the answers to the questions "What kind of Messiah?" and "What does it take to be a follower of this Christ?" Throughout, those who are supposed to be Jesus' closest disciples seem to understand nothing of what he says, particularly about his passion. Immediately following Peter's proclamation of Jesus as the Messiah, Mark relays that Jesus "began to teach them that the Son of Man must undergo great suffering and be rejected by the elders, the chief priests, and the scribes, and be killed, and after three days rise again" (8:31). Peter, not understanding at all, rejects this notion of messiahship (8:32).

The next incident recounted by Mark is the transfiguration (9:2-8). Peter, James, and John—three of Jesus' most intimate friends—are privy to a revelatory experience concerning Jesus' identity. But Mark shows them as uncomprehending, mistakenly putting Jesus, Moses, and Elijah on the same plane. Following this is the story of the disciples' inability to cast out a demon from a young boy (9:14-29), adding to an unflattering picture of those we would expect to best emulate Jesus.

A second time Jesus teaches his disciples about his coming passion (9:30-32). "But they did not understand what he was saying, and were afraid to ask him" (9:32). To highlight just how little they comprehended, Mark immediately describes how the disciples were arguing among themselves about who was the greatest (9:33-37). Reinforcing his picture of bumbling disciples, Mark relates how Jesus became indignant with them when they turned away the children (10:13-16), and how amazed the disciples were when Jesus taught that it was very difficult for those with wealth to enter the reign of God (10:23-31).

A third time, while journeying to Jerusalem, Jesus takes the disciples aside and tells them what is about to happen to him (10:32-34). Once again they miss the point, as demonstrated by the next episode (10:35-45), with James and John vying for the seats at Jesus' right and left when he comes in glory.

All through the Gospel, these intimates of Jesus are slow to understand and, at times, even seem to oppose Jesus. The reader of Mark's Gospel wonders whether there is any hope that the disciples will ever understand who Jesus is and what they are to do as his followers. In the passion narrative, the failure of the disciples escalates. They fall asleep during Jesus' struggle in Gethsemane (14:32-42). Judas, one of the Twelve, betrays Jesus (14:43-52). Those who left all to follow him (1:16-20) leave him and flee at his arrest (14:50). And their supposed leader, Peter, denies he even knew Jesus (14:66-72).

Mark makes it eminently clear that full understanding of Jesus and his message is not what qualifies one for a graced encounter with him or for discipleship. In every instance grace begins with God and is a gift freely given to human beings, mediated through Jesus. All that is necessary is the gift of faith and a willingness to follow Jesus and participate in his mission. As the disciples in the Gospel of Mark demonstrate, no one ever fully understands this call.

Stages of Understanding in the Gospel of John

The fourth evangelist best illustrates the process by which a person is led by Jesus into a deeper understanding of who he is. With dramatic flair, John tells stories in which characters move from ignorance to knowledge. One such story is that of the man born blind (John 9:1-41). John presents this drama in six scenes. He begins by telling us that Jesus was passing by when he saw a man blind from birth. A discussion between Jesus and his disciples intervenes (vv. 2-5, to which we will return). Then Jesus ''spat on the ground and made mud with the saliva, and spread the mud on the man's eyes, saying to him, 'Go, wash in the pool of Siloam' (which means Sent). Then he went and washed and came back able to see'' (vv. 6-7).

It is remarkable that, unlike other healing stories in the Gospels, the man born blind does not initiate the encounter with Jesus. He does not seem to know anything about Jesus or to have asked for anything from him. The grace of God comes to him despite his previous lack of perception. Each of the following five scenes shows how Jesus leads him deeper and deeper into understanding.

The second scene (vv. 8-12) involves his neighbors and those who had seen him earlier as a beggar. They ask him how his eyes were opened and he responds, "The man called Jesus made mud, spread it on my eyes, and said to me, 'Go to Siloam and wash.' Then I went and washed and received my sight" (v. 11). When they further press him, "Where is he?" he replies, "I do not know." The question of Jesus' whereabouts is closely related to the question of who Jesus is (see also John 7:11-12). The man who was cured gives a minimal identification of the one who healed him: all he knows is that the man is called Jesus; he does not know where he is. He has a long way to go before reaching full faith in Jesus.

In the next scene (vv. 13-17) the Pharisees interrogate the man who had been blind. Once again he explains how he can now see. The Pharisees begin to debate among themselves whether Jesus is from God. Some say, "This man is not from God, for he does not observe the Sabbath." Others say, "How can a man who is a sinner perform such signs?" (v. 16). They turn again to the man who had been healed, asking, "What do you say about him? It was your eyes he opened." He said, "He is a prophet" (v. 17). With this statement, the man has moved a bit further in his understanding of Jesus. Prophets are people who are especially close to God and who speak and act with God's authority. The man who was healed recognizes that Jesus has such power.

In the next vignette (vv. 18-23), the Pharisees interrogate the parents of the man who was healed. All that they will divulge are the obvious facts: ". . . we do not know how it is that now he sees, nor do we know who opened his eyes. Ask him; he is of age. He will speak for himself" (v. 21). The desire of the parents to be dissociated from Jesus stands in contrast to the developing faith of their son.

Scene five (vv. 24-34) brings the man who had been blind back on stage to face the Pharisees once again. The latter have solidified their position that Jesus is a sinner. The man replies, ''I do not know whether he is a sinner. One thing I do know, that though I was blind, now I see'' (v. 25). As the Pharisees press him to tell again how it happened, the healed man, reluctant to repeat his story, finally asks, ''Do you also want to become his disciples?'' (v. 27). He further asserts that Jesus is from God because of what he is able to do (v. 33). The Pharisees respond indignantly and throw him out.

It is striking that the man does not seem to have progressed any further in his understanding of Jesus. He says he does not know if Jesus is a sinner. But he does know that Jesus has made him see. Then he concludes that Jesus is from God, just as he did during his first interrogation by the Pharisees when he asserted that Jesus is a prophet (v. 17). The healed man seems at first to have regressed—but as he works it through again, he concludes anew that Jesus is from God.

Despite his shortcomings, the cured man has become a disciple of Jesus. This man is not theologically well informed nor articulate. Even what he once knew about Jesus he has to discover again. The one thing he does well is to relate his own experience of Jesus. He knows that he was blind and now he sees (vv. 11, 15, 25). He knows who made that happen. He eventually comes to the decision that Jesus is from God, but he does not have the skills to win over the Pharisees with his witness. Though he does not have a very sophisticated understanding of Jesus, he knows he has encountered God through him, and can commit himself to being his disciple. He suffers the consequences of discipleship: he is expelled from the synagogue.

The sixth scene brings the healed man and Jesus together again (vv. 35-39). Jesus, hearing that the Pharisees had thrown him out, looks for the man and brings him another step in his understanding. Jesus asks, ''Do you believe in the Son of Man?'' (v. 35). The man replies, ''And who is he, sir? Tell me, so that I may believe in him'' (v. 36). Either he doesn't understand the meaning of ''Son of Man'' or he doesn't know how to identify this figure. In any case, what stands out is his readiness to believe. Jesus, who enabled him to have physical sight, now helps him to have more fully developed eyes of faith. "You have seen him, and the one speaking with you is he" (v. 37). The man gives the perfect response, " 'Lord, I believe' and he worshipped him" (v. 38).

This is the story of a person who, through no merit of his own, comes to a profound faith and understanding of Jesus. The initial impulse comes from Jesus. What is required of the man is the willingness to believe. It is Jesus himself, who, through repeated encounters, draws the man into deeper knowledge of God.

The story of the Samaritan woman in John 4:1-42 is very similar. Again, Jesus initiates the encounter by asking the woman for a drink (v. 7). At first, all that she recognizes about Jesus is that he is a Jew (v. 8). He will lead her to see the "gift of God" (v. 10) that he offers. In her first tentative step toward faith in Jesus, she asks, "Are you greater than our ancestor Jacob, who gave us the well?" (v. 12). Even though she misunderstands Jesus' response about "living water" (v. 10), she exhibits the same willingness as the man healed from blindness when she says, "Sir, give me this water, so that I may never be thirsty or have to keep coming here to draw water" (v. 15). She, too, recognizes Jesus as a prophet (v. 19) when he speaks about her husbands. Bit by bit Jesus leads her to the revelation that he is the Messiah for whom she is waiting (vv. 25-26). Like the fishermen who leave their nets to follow him (Mark 1:16-20), she leaves her water jar to tell the townspeople about him (v. 28).

An important aspect of this story is that this person whom Jesus leads into faith is both a woman and a Samaritan. As John informs his readers, Jews and Samaritans have nothing to do with each other (v. 9). The reaction of Jesus' disciples, who return from town with food, bespeaks the typical attitude of their day toward women: "Why are you speaking with her?" (v. 27). If intellectual theological education were a prerequisite for encountering Jesus, then Jesus should be most successful among the Jewish religious leaders and the theologically educated men of his day. However, all four Gospels portray the religious leaders as uniformly opposed to Jesus. It is

GREG'S RELUCTANCE ABOUT THE BLOOD

Greg and his family belong to an active parish. Children are used to gathering around the altar after the presentation of the gifts and Greg is one of the first to be close to the pastor. And he is one of the last to return to his seat at the passing of the peace because he wants to hug everyone. When Greg was twelve years old, his family enrolled him in a special catechetical group to ready him for first Communion. Although he attended the class regularly, he refused to eat with the group. He would wrap his cookies to take home. And every time the class would gather, Greg would insist that he did not like to drink blood. After two years, Greg was finally willing to eat cookies and sing with his group. Even though he continued to refuse to drink the wine, Greg participated in first Communion in his own way, using one of his cookies as a wafer.

women—who, according to the attitudes of Jesus' day, would not be expected to understand—that are entrusted with the message of the resurrection! Furthermore, in Mark's Gospel it is a Roman centurion, a Gentile, who makes the most profound profession of faith at Jesus' death: "Truly this man was God's Son!" (15:39). He articulates what no disciple has been able to grasp throughout the whole of Mark's story.

The Faith of the Community

John's Gospel highlights the development of relationships between Jesus and individuals. The man healed of blindness seems to stand alone against his parents, neighbors, and the religious leaders as he embarks upon a faith journey with Jesus. The Samaritan woman, too, is a solitary figure as she comes to the well at an hour when she is unlikely to meet other women. Only after a significant development in her relationship with Jesus does the rest of the community enter. It is part of John's style to portray representative characters in such a way that anyone in similar circumstances can identify with them. Because of John's emphasis on symbolic individuals the role of the whole faith community is downplayed in his stories. The importance of the believing community is best illustrated in an episode in Mark 2:1-12.[2]

Mark tells how once, when Jesus was at home preaching in Capernaum, so many people had gathered that there was not even room around the door. Four people came, carrying their friend who was paralyzed. Unable to get near Jesus because of the crowd, they opened up the roof above him. After they had broken through, they let down the mat on which their friend was lying. When Jesus saw their faith, he said to the one who was paralyzed, "Son, your sins are forgiven" (Mark 2:4-5). In this story, the graced encounter of Jesus and the man who was paralyzed depends completely on the faith of his friends. It is they who carry him, physically and spiritually. It is their faith that Jesus sees. Also, in Mark 7:32, "people" bring to Jesus a man who had hearing and speech impediments and beg Jesus to lay his hand on him. So too, at Bethsaida, "some people" bring to Jesus a man who was blind and beg Jesus to touch him (Mark 8:22).

These stories made eminent sense to a first-century Mediterranean audience. Contrary to our understanding of the person as a unique individual capable of relating to others, persons of Jesus' day defined their very selves by the communities to which they belonged. This is called dyadic personality, wherein every individual identity is embedded in some other (Malina 1993, 63–89). Paul gives us a good example of this in Philippians 3:5. In presenting his defense of the gospel he preaches, Paul identifies himself according to the groups in which he is embedded: "Circumcised on the eighth day, a member of the people of Israel, of the tribe of Benjamin, a Hebrew born of Hebrews; as to the law, a Pharisee." In terms of the dyadic personality, it is not the faith of the man who is paralyzed that gains him access to Jesus, but rather the faith of the community to which he belongs. Furthermore, at the end of the story, Jesus tells him to go home (v. 11), implying that through his forgiveness and physical healing, wholeness and holiness are restored to his entire community.

Impurity As Obstacle to Access

There are stories in the Gospels in which persons with physical or mental afflictions appear outcast and marginalized from their communities. In such narratives, the person seeking access to Jesus has to overcome immense obstacles to reach him. One such incident occurs in Mark 5:25-34:

> There was a woman afflicted with hemorrhages for twelve years. She had suffered greatly at the hands of many doctors and had spent all she had. Yet she was not helped but only grew worse. She had heard about Jesus and came up behind him in the crowd and touched his cloak. She said, "If I but touch his clothes, I shall be cured." Immediately her flow of blood dried up. She felt in her body that she was healed of her affliction. Jesus, aware at once that power had gone out from him, turned around in the crowd and asked, "Who touched my clothes?" But his disciples said to him, "You see how the crowd is pressing upon you, and yet you

ask, 'Who touched me?' '' And he looked around to see who
had done it. The woman, realizing what had happened to
her, approached in fear and trembling. She fell down before Jesus and told him the whole truth. He said to her,
"Daughter, your faith has saved you. Go in peace and be
cured of your affliction" (NAB).

The obstacles this woman faces seem almost insurmount-
able. Her hemorrhaging must have made her physically debilitated. Her economic resources are now depleted. Her spirit,
as well, must be sorely tried, as her hopes are dashed time after
time, seeking help from one doctor after another. But the most
devastating must have been her marginalization from her religious community and family. In Leviticus 15:25-27 the Law
states:

> When a woman is afflicted with a flow of blood for several
> days outside her menstrual period, or when her flow con-
> tinues beyond the ordinary period, as long as she suffers this
> unclean flow she shall be unclean, just as during her men-
> strual period. Any bed on which she lies during such a flow
> becomes unclean, as it would during her menstruation, and
> any article of furniture on which she sits becomes unclean
> just as during her menstruation. Anyone who touches them
> becomes unclean; he shall wash his garments, bathe in water,
> and be unclean until evening (NAB).

Purity laws such as these were designed to ensure the holiness of the community by clearly delineating the boundaries
between clean and unclean (see Bergant above; Malina 1993,
149–83). Persons with abnormal bodily flows or skin disorders
were considered anomalous. They were not considered whole
and could not symbolize wholeness or perfection before God.
They were, therefore, disqualified from Temple worship or sacrifice. Moreover, the entire holy land replicated the holy space
of God symbolized by the Temple. Consequently, an unclean
person, such as the woman with hemorrhages, was seen to
be unfit for ordinary social intercourse. The community, rather
than serve as a vehicle for her restoration—as with the man
who was paralyzed—views her with horror and fear as unclean
and unholy, and relegates her to its fringes.

Jesus' Interpretation of Purity

It is precisely the people considered unclean and unholy that Jesus seeks out: people with leprosy (Mark 1:40-45; Luke 17:11-19), people thought to be possessed by demons (Mark 1:21-28; 5:1-20); people who were blind (Mark 8:22-26; 10:46-52), people who were paralyzed (Mark 2:1-12); people with hearing and speech impairments (Mark 7:31-37). Jesus' practice of healing people with such disabilities on the Sabbath (e.g., Mark 1:21-27; 3:1-6) provoked confrontations with the religious leaders. In debating with them on the meaning of the Sabbath, Jesus does not reject the purpose of the Jewish purity system; rather he questions whether it is being properly interpreted and implemented according to its purpose: to facilitate access to God. When he says to the Pharisees, "The Sabbath was made for humankind, not humankind for the Sabbath" (Mark 2:27), he is saying, in effect, that purity regulations should facilitate access to God, not bar God's people from access to the holy. The central concern should be God's will, which is the wholeness and holiness of God's people; not the maintenance of the purity system for its own sake (Malina 1993, 172–81). The woman who suffered from hemorrhages experiences a sacramental encounter with Jesus when the Pharisees bar her from access to the holy. Jesus' address to her, "Daughter," (Mark 5:34) reincorporates her into full participation in the family of Israel.

In all of the healing stories in the Gospels, a graced encounter with Jesus restores a person to *shalom*, to fullness of health and well-being on every level. There is no longer any impediment in terms of purity regulations for their approaching the holy. But what about access to the holy and full integration into the faith community for those whose "impurities" are not removed? Jesus' deliberate association with such persons is undoubtedly the most objectionable aspect of his ministry. Time and again, particularly in the Gospel of Luke, Jesus is seen eating with persons considered "unclean," such as an unhealed leper (Mark 14:3) or unrepentant tax collectors and sinners (e.g., Luke 5:30; 7:34; 15:2; 19:7). Tax collectors, such as Levi (Luke 5:27-32), sitting at his customs post in Capernaum, would be in a perpetual state of uncleanness because of constant contact with Gentiles. "Sinners" were of two sorts: Jews who transgressed the Law, who could repent and be fully reintegrated into the holy people of God; and Gentiles, who would always be "sinners" since they did not even know the Law.

Jesus' practice of eating with such people incurs the ire of the other religious leaders. Eating together symbolizes sharing life together. It is an affront to the purity regulations when the boundaries between clean and unclean are ignored in such meal sharing. Furthermore, a meal symbolizes the sharing of God's life together in the eschatological reign of God. The prophet Isaiah describes the messianic banquet:

> On this mountain the LORD of hosts will provide for all peoples a feast of rich food and choice wines, juicy, rich food and pure, choice wines. On this mountain he will destroy the veil that veils all peoples, the web that is woven over all nations; he will destroy death forever. The Lord GOD will wipe away the tears from all faces; the reproach of his people he will remove from the whole earth; for the LORD has spoken (Isa 25:6-8, NAB).

Thus, Jesus' eating with tax collectors and sinners not only challenges the interpretation of the purity regulations of his day, but also symbolizes who will be included in the realm of God at the end times.

Jesus' Chosen Self-Identification

The most radical step of all is not simply that Jesus associates with those considered unclean, but that Jesus himself assumes such an identity. In doing so, Jesus redefines the notions of "holy" and "unholy."

Let us return for a moment to the story of the man who was born blind in John 9. It opens with a question posed by Jesus' disciples: "Rabbi, who sinned, this man or his parents, that he was born blind?" (v. 2). The disciples' question reflects the age-old belief in a direct causal relationship between sin and suffering. Despite the lessons of Job, the only alternatives they envision are either that the man himself sinned, or that he is suffering for the sin of his parents. There are a number of instances in the First Testament that testify to the latter belief (e.g., Exod 20:5; Deut 5:9; Sir 41:5-7; Job 4:7; 8:4, 20). Ezekiel, however, puts forth the idea that people suffer only for their own sins (Ezek 18:19-20). Jesus' answer allows for neither possibility: "Neither this man nor his parents sinned; he was born blind so that God's works might be revealed through him" (John 9:2-3). Jesus gives no further answer as to the cause of suffering, but what is sure is that it is not punishment for sin. A similar saying is found in Luke 13:1-3, where Jesus is told about "the Galileans whose blood Pilate had mingled with their sacrifices." Jesus' reply is, "Do you think that because these Galileans suffered in this way they were worse sinners than all other Galileans? No, I tell you . . . ."

In addition, then, to being socially and religiously marginalized by purity regulations, people with physical and mental disabilities were regarded as sinners, whose suffering was a sign of punishment from God. The sayings of Jesus in Luke 13 and John 9 deny such an understanding of disability. Yet these sayings are not Jesus' final word on the topic. In his own actions, in his own body, he identified with the marginalized and those with disabilities. Some thought him to be mentally imbalanced. Mark says that his relatives "went out to restrain him, for people were saying, 'He has gone out of his mind' " (3:21). The scribes from Jerusalem thought him possessed by Beelzebul (Mark 3:22). Aside from these projections of others, Jesus willingly took on a broken and disabled body as he died a criminal's death of crucifixion. Through his passion, death, and resurrection, Jesus transformed a broken body from a sign of rejection and punishment by God to the very symbol of salvation. The Law declares, "anyone hung on a tree is under God's curse" (Deut 21:23). But the good news is that Jesus' broken body signifies blessing, and opens the way for the inclusion of all people with "impurities" who might otherwise be denied access to the holy. Paul declares, "For our sake he [God] made him to be sin who knew no sin, so that in him we might become the righteousness of God" (2 Cor 5:21). And again, "Christ redeemed us from the curse of the law by becoming a curse for us" (Gal 3:13). As in the story of the man who had been born blind, the works of God are made most visible through one who would appear to be unholy.

It is not when one is made "whole" or "clean" that one most closely emulates the holiness of Jesus. Returning to the story of the woman who suffered from hemorrhages, we see that Mark takes pains to paint her in parallel strokes to Jesus when he describes her before she is healed. He says she has "suffered greatly" (Mark 5:26). In Greek the verb is *paschō*, the same verb Jesus uses in Mark 8:31 and 9:12 to describe to his disciples the suffering he will undergo in the passion. In verses 29 and 34 her suffering is referred to as "affliction." The Greek word *mastix* literally means "scourge," the same word Jesus uses in Mark 10:34 as he tells his disciples what will befall him at the hands of the religious leaders in Jerusalem.

Conclusion

Reflecting on these gospel stories can aid us in shaping our attitudes and practices toward persons with disabilities in our own faith communities. The initiative comes from Jesus. The person who experiences the sacramental encounter has no previous preparation and no specific qualifications. Graced encounters with Jesus are a free gift. Those with developmental disabilities remind all of us that no one earns access to God.

We have also seen that theological acumen is not a condition for ongoing discipleship. Jesus' most intimate followers show little or no understanding of who he is or the gospel he proclaims. What is required of every disciple is a willingness to believe (John 9:36) and to follow Jesus to the fullness of one's capacity. Not all were able to follow to the cross (Mark 14:50); not all were able to proclaim the good news (Mark 16:8).

This is not to devalue theological education; nor is it to say that catechesis for sacramental encounters is unnecessary. Rather, it is essential that we engage in the type of catechesis that recognizes the different modes of knowing and celebrating pertinent to those with developmental disabilities. One effective method involves reflection on what has been experienced in the sacrament, rather than concentration on the articulation of theological concepts before reception is permitted

GENERAL CONFESSION AND ABSOLUTION IS NOT ENOUGH

Eight mentally handicapped adults and nine catechists had been together for six years in one community of faith before they began to talk about celebrating the sacrament of penance together. Five of the handicapped are severely retarded and do not speak. Even so, they know how to convey sorrow to one another, to forgive and be forgiven. They followed form no. 3 (reconciliation of several penitents with general confession and absolution) as they prepared for a celebration in Advent. The focus of their preparations was on the bonds among them, what it meant to be forgiven and then be friends again. The pastor who had been asked to preside at the sacrament of penance insisted on individual confession and absolution.

(Harrington 1991). This approach would be in tune with the way in which Jesus led people like the Samaritan woman and the man born blind into a deeper understanding of himself. Jesus draws on what they have experienced of him in the tangible, concrete, bodily, affective, and spontaneous realities of everyday life to bring them to further understanding. These are the very modes to which those with developmental disabilities are best attuned.

In some of the gospel stories a person who suffers from a disability already has faith and takes the initiative, overcoming great obstacles to reach Jesus. Bartimaeus, blind, and begging at the side of the road, cries out over a crowd that tries to silence him (Mark 10:46-52). The woman who was hemorrhaging defies physical, economic, social, and religious taboos to grab the fringe of Jesus' cloak (Mark 5:25-34). In these instances, Jesus approves their efforts and affirms, "your faith has saved you" (Mark 5:34; 10:52).

We are embarrassed for Jesus' disciples, who create one more obstacle as they say, "You see how the crowd is pressing upon you, and yet you ask, 'Who touched me?' " (Mark 5:31). They don't understand: "Why are you speaking with her?" (John 4:27). They stand in the way of "children" who come to Jesus (Mark 10:13-16). The Jewish religious leaders, too, repeatedly interrogate those Jesus healed (John 9:13-17, 24-34), and challenge his disciples (Mark 2:16) and Jesus himself (Mark 2:24). The very ones who should facilitate access to the holy impede it. Religious leaders today will not want to be found standing in the way of Jesus' invitation to persons with disabilities. Rather, they must be committed to a vision of Church in which such persons are included, belong, and participate to the fullest extent possible.

We have recalled gospel stories in which individuals are not capable of coming to Jesus on their own. In these instances, the community carries the person to a graced encounter. Like the four friends of the man who was paralyzed (Mark 2:1-12), the faith community bears up each member. And it is the entire community that encounters Jesus in the sacraments. The capabilities of the entire community—and not an individual believer—are the criteria for admission.

Finally, when we reflect on Jesus' chosen self-identification with persons in their brokenness, there remains no question about persons with developmental disabilities having access to the sacraments. The body of Christ is not composed of whole and holy persons who charitably admit people with disabilities into this graced arena. Rather, the body of Christ is one that is broken and rejected. Genuine encounter with the holy is possible only when every member of the body, with his or her brokenness, is included and participates fully, using his or her particular gifts in ministry. Paul says this best:

> Indeed, the body does not consist of one member but of many. If the foot would say, "Because I am not a hand I do not belong to the body," that would not make it any less a part of the body. And if the ear would say, "Because I am not an eye I do not belong to the body," that would not make it any less a part of the body. If the whole body were an eye, where would the hearing be? If the whole body were hearing, where would the sense of smell be? But as it is, God arranged the members in the body, each one of them, as he chose. If all were a single member, where would the body be? As it is, there are many members, yet one body. The eye cannot say to the hand, "I have no need of you," nor again the head to the feet, "I have no need of you." On the contrary, the members of the body that seem to be weaker are indispensable, and those members of the body that we think less honorable we clothe with greater honor, and our less respectable members are treated with greater respect; whereas our more respectable members do not need this. But God has so arranged the body, giving the greater honor to the inferior member, that there may be no dissension within the body, but the members may have the same care for one another. If one members suffers, all suffer together with it; if one member is honored, all rejoice together with it (1 Cor 12:14-26).

NOTES

1. All Biblical quotations are from the New Revised Standard Version unless it is noted that they are from the New American Bible [NAB].

2. See John Huels' treatment of sacraments as ecclesial acts below.

REFERENCES

Harrington, Mary Therese. *A Place for All: Mental Retardation, Catechesis and Liturgy.* American Essays in Liturgy. Collegeville: The Liturgical Press, 1991.

Malina, B. *The New Testament World. Insights From Cultural Anthropology.* Rev. ed. Atlanta: John Knox, 1993. See especially "The First-Century Personality: The Individual and the Group," 63–89; "Clean and Unclean: Understanding Rules of Purity," 149–83.

FURTHER READING

Gaventa, William. "Religious Ministries and Services with Adults with Developmental Disabilities." In *The Right to Grow Up. An Introduction to Adults with Developmental Disabilities.* Baltimore: Paul H. Brookes, 1986. Pp. 191–226. This article assesses the religious needs of adults with developmental disabilities and the barriers that hinder their religious involvement. It provides a fine overview of practical guidelines and theological considerations for the full inclusion of such persons in the faith community.

Karris, Robert. "God's Boundary Breaking Mercy." *The Bible Today* 24 (1986) 24–29. Karris explores Luke's good news of God's boundary-breaking mercy from three perspectives: Jesus' miracles, his table companionship with outcasts, and his teachings on the dangers of greed and on love of enemies.

Moloney, Francis. *A Body Broken for a Broken People: Eucharist in the New Testament.* Melbourne: Collins Dove, 1990. This volume traces the beginnings of our Eucharistic tradition in each of the four Gospels and in Paul's Letters to the Corinthians. Moloney finds that all have a fundamental idea of the Eucharist as the presence of Jesus to the broken, and challenges the Church to ask whether current practice and theology is at one with this gospel message.

Selvidge, Marla. "Mark 5:25-34 and Leviticus 15:19-20." *Journal of Biblical Literature* 103 (1984) 619–23. Selvidge argues that Mark preserves a tradition that subtly shatters the legal purity system, such as that found in Leviticus 15:19-20. The emphasis in Mark 5:25-34 is not on restricting women but on preserving stories of how they were liberated from physical and social suffering.

Senior, Donald. "Suffering as Inaccessibility." *New Theology Review* 1 (1988) 5–14. The author shows how, in the gospel stories of healing, Jesus eradicates the suffering that results from denial of access to full participation in the faith community. Such stories direct Christians to see their mission as commitment to gaining dignity, respect, and full access for all God's daughters and sons.

3

Pondering the Anomaly of God's Love

Ethical Reflections on Access to the Sacraments

Paul J. Wadell, C.P.

A Christmas Story

"A child is born to us, a son is given us," but it was not the son they expected. Two months early and gasping for life, this Christmas morning gift took them by surprise and turned their lives inside out. His manger was a small, flat table in the neonatal unit where children are not expected to survive. He was not wrapped in swaddling clothes but in needles, tape, and tubes that covered every inch of his innocent flesh. One look at him brought one to reverence and softened one's heart. Stalked by death and wounded by a life that began too soon, to behold him was to encounter holiness, to come before the presence of God and be awed. As the shepherds and the wise gathered around the Christ child to ponder the mystery of God's great love, this was Christ's child too. In this tiny gift, utterly helpless and shockingly needy, humanity and God came together again. God was lying there, fighting for life, pleading for the world's recognition; it was an incarnation, another Christmas morning.

The child's name is Carl. He was born with cerebral palsy and he is my nephew. But on that Christmas morning he was also a sacrament, God speaking to us in cryptic, saving ways. Hidden in an affliction that would mark him for life was a word worth hearing, a grace ready to redeem. Like every sacrament, this outward sign of rebellious muscles and determined heart bore a secret gospel. God was in this fragile flower, beckoning to us with some astonishing news about things human and divine. In this Christmas morning gift, transparent with neediness too flagrant to be denied, was a surprising, liberating gospel about God and ourselves. Here was not one of the strong, but a child of sacred incompleteness. Here was a beloved of God with frailty and fracture that could not be disguised. Here was God where we least expected: hidden away in the lowly, shrouded in the harmless who disturb. It is through such misbegotten that God speaks to us the most.

The eloquence of God is often embodied in those whom we tend to dismiss. We think of persons with developmental disabilities as anomalies. If they are sacraments,[1] however, manifestations of God and manifestations of ourselves, perhaps the real deviants are those who fail to heed the message they convey. This is a book about access to the sacraments for persons in the Church with disabilities, but in order to understand how to address that question we need to turn things around. What if those with developmental disabilities are sacraments of God's life and it is we, the allegedly able-bodied, who must first have access to them? We will never understand our obligations in justice to persons with disabilities unless we scrutinize what they reveal about God and ourselves.

We begin with heads turned and hearts opened. Our focus in assessing who should have access to God in the sacraments is not on the people we take to be normal, but on the needy ones in our midst who stray from the norm just as much as our God does. To understand rightly what access to the sacraments means, we must begin with those who mirror best both God and ourselves. Disabled persons reflect back to us a different understanding of ourselves and a different understanding of God. In pondering that reflection we learn why access to the sacraments in the Church is something determined by God, not ourselves. In this chapter, we shall examine this question of sacramental access for persons with disabilities by asking (1) what do people with physical and mental disabilities teach us about ourselves? (2) what do they teach us about God and what God wants for us? and (3) what do they teach us about what it means to be the Church?

Befriending the Ones We Usually Exclude

We must begin not by discussing but by befriending. In order to understand the moral dimensions of access to the sacraments for persons in the Church with developmental disabilities, the critical first step is to befriend the ones we normally exclude, or perhaps better, to allow them to befriend us. In Christopher Nolan's poignant and beautiful autobiographical novel *Under the Eye of the Clock*, Joseph Meehan, born mute and crippled, writes of Alex Clark, "who belonged to that great able-bodied world" (Nolan 1987, 4), and who "devoted time and trouble to not only pushing Joseph's wheelchair, but to being one of Joseph's acute and early friends." Meehan remembers how "Alex brought his strength into play and sacking Joseph's cross of much of its sting . . . helped his friend to sample some of the good things of life" (Nolan 1987, 5). Through Alex "he captured again the security felt when a mute crippled boy has a brave vocal friend" (Nolan 1987, 6).

But what happens to the able-bodied when they receive the offer of friendship that comes from the mute and the crippled? If Joseph Meehan was able to share in the world of the able-bodied through the kindness of Alex Clark, then it is through friendship with the Joseph Meehan's of this world that we enter the world of those we seldom take time to understand. If we are not to be handicapped by our fear of those who initially seem so different, we have to cross a boundary and risk entering their world. Being befriended by persons with disabilities is like entering another country. It is foreign terrain; its landscape looks so different. We are confronted by alien customs. We meet people with a novel understanding of what it means to be. It is unsettling, but we must be willing to listen to them and learn from them. Being open to the friendship of those we normally avoid is essential for discovering what God wants for all of us and what it means to treat such people justly.

Persons with disabilities force us to think of ourselves differently. Entering their world, our self is reflected back to us in ways we normally do not glimpse or work hard to obscure. More than anything, they show us that we are persons of individuality and strength not when we are autonomous and self-sufficient, but, in M. Scott Peck's marvelous phrase, when we learn "the power of helplessness" (Peck 1990, 77). As Stephen Solaris, the brain-damaged, bedridden prophet of Peck's novel *A Bed by the Window* reminds us, those who are powerful are those who have "come to terms with their helplessness" (Peck 1990, 78).

The idea that the powerful and the strong are those who have embraced their helplessness offers us a different understanding of what it means to be a person. It may also be the most significant gift the disabled bring us. Human beings are those who have come to grips with their need, not ashamed to confess their indigence and no longer embarrassed by inabilities. This is the first lesson about personhood we learn when we enter the world of those people we normally fear. We cannot be persons unless we know our helplessness and acknowledge our need. Anything else is a dangerous deception. Once we accept the power of our helplessness we begin to understand why persons with disabilities are a metaphor for all of us; indeed, we realize that if we see them as an anomaly it is only because we profoundly misunderstand ourselves.

Sometimes we want to misunderstand because we fear what the truth reveals. Perhaps we exclude the disabled and refuse to grant them access to our lives and our communities because we do not want to accept what they tell us about ourselves. Their disabilities frighten us not because we do not know how to help them belong, but because being with them discloses how false and misguided is the dominant understanding of ourselves. And so we work to construct a world that vetoes their presence and overrules their pleas to belong. We do this under the pretext of protecting them from harm, but the truth may be that we want to protect ourselves from what they have to teach us. In *Under the Eye of the Clock*, Joseph Meehan reflects on this strategy of exclusion when he learns his application for school has once again been rejected:

> Someone always vetoes his application thought Joseph . . . someone always vetoes; someone normal; someone beautiful; someone blessed by normality; someone administering the rusty mind's rules of yesteryear; . . . someone Christian worst of all, boasted ascetic, one of the head-strokers-poor child, God love him, ah God is good, never shuts one door but he opens another; . . . someone versed in the art of saying no; . . . someone able to say no to a dumb cripple; someone always says no (Nolan 1987, 12–13).

Unmasking a Heretical View of the Self

The last thing we want is to learn the power of our helplessness. Our culture promotes an anthropology that says to be human is to be "free from all unanswered needs" (McGill 1987, 14). We rebel against limitations, refuse to be deflected by the unexpected, and insist that any incompleteness can be overcome. Our normative view of the self suggests an ideology of the strong. More often than not, we believe we can be fulfilled in all our capacities, constantly growing and never diminishing, lacking nothing and in masterful control of our lives. In the ideology of the strong, frailty is not accepted as part of the human condition, nor is misfortune or tragedy; such unhappiness comes only to those who plan poorly or choose wrongly. There is no room for failure in the ideology of the strong; indeed, "a person must try to prove by his or her own existence that failure does not belong essentially to life" (McGill 1987, 18).

This is the understanding of self dominating Western culture, and it helps us understand why the unhidden frailty of the disabled is such an affront. In the ideology of the strong, the "normal" person shows no sign of debility and acknowledges no helplessness. Arthur McGill calls such persons the "bronze people" (McGill 1987, 26). In the ideology of the strong, they are paradigms of human flourishing. The bronze people are never deflected by chance or ravaged by misfortune; indeed, they betray not the slightest hint of incompletion. With

them "all traces of weakness, debility, ugliness, and helplessness must be kept away from every part of a person's life"
(McGill 1987, 26). Disabled by nothing, they live by their own
power and include others by choice but never by need. As
Stanley Hauerwas reflects: "We seek to be strong. We seek
to be self-possessed. We seek to deny that we depend on others
for our existence. We will be self-reliant and we resent and
avoid those who do not seek to be like us—the strong"
(Hauerwas 1986, 175).

This vision of personhood which dominates our culture il-
luminates why anyone less than perfectly whole is a scandal.
The most obvious truth about persons with mental or physical disabilities is that they are not creatures of total self-
possession, but persons who clearly depend on others. They
live from their neediness; everything about them communicates their dependence on people who care and are willing to
love. But bronze people depend on no one. Their identity
comes not from the relationships they have with others, but
from their self-sufficiency. They could never understand Joseph
Meehan's whispered prayer, "Do with me what you can. . . .
I can be but my feeble self" (Nolan 1987, 25), because they
could never countenance such an unabashed confession of
need.

We exclude persons with disabilities from our midst because
they unmask the pretensions with which we live. We label
them as disabled or retarded or deviant not because they are
less than human, but because to accept them would be to learn
that our sense of normalcy must be radically revised. They
show us how little we know about what it means to be human
and challenge us to turn from ignorance by learning from them.
We need access to them much more than they to us because
in our self-deception we hardly realize how disabling the ideology of the strong really is.

Perhaps the greatest injustice inflicted on persons with disabilities is to exclude them not for their sake but for ours. We
keep them at a distance because we do not want to see that
we too are helpless and needy; our lives too are fragile, vul-
nerable, and assailable by chance. Because those with disabilities expose our definitions of normalcy as pathetically

misguided, we label them in a way that justifies their exclusion. We call them disabled not because they are helpless, but because they are so glaringly other than what we think a normal person should be. What they refuse to hide scares us. We fail to grant them access to our lives—and sometimes even to God—because we are profoundly uncomfortable with the realities they symbolize. They offend us because they are willing to be what we fear:

> Even worse, they do not try to hide their needs. They are not self-sufficient, they are not self-possessed, they are in need. Even more, they do not evidence the proper shame for being so. They simply assume that they are what they are and they need to provide no justification for being such. It is almost as if they have been given a natural grace to be free from the regret most of us feel for our neediness (Hauerwas 1986, 176).

Human Life Is a Resting-in-Neediness

Persons with disabilities bring a different sense of what is normal. Their lives testify that the most inescapable fact about being human is to be in need. This does not mean that the disabled are initially more accepting of their neediness than anyone else, for indeed they can resist it as well as the rest of us; however, their lives show us that being in need is not a disability, but a fundamental fact of being human which all of us are ultimately unable—and should have no desire—to hide.[2] Arthur McGill poignantly summarizes this perspective by suggesting that "human life is a resting-in-neediness" (McGill 1987, 83). No one teaches this better than those in our midst with needs too glaring to suppress. As Dianne Bergant suggests at the end of her essay in this volume, persons with disabilities do not see neediness as something to escape but as the starting point for understanding rightly who we are. We begin to know ourselves when we acknowledge our indigence, when we confess the incompleteness at the core of our being.

Unlike the bronze people, persons with disabilities espouse an anthropology which says each of us is inescapably incomplete and unavoidably dependent on others for our existence.

BIANCA HAS A MIND OF HER OWN

Bianca was nine when she first came for catechesis. She was disruptive and violent. She would kick and yell and try to climb on the altar when the community gathered to worship. Bianca was contrary and stubborn. Because of her lack of verbal communication and her stubbornness and because the group she joined had been together for two years, Bianca was quickly isolated. She was withdrawn from the group.

After two years, Bianca's parents asked again if she could join a group for catechesis. She was able to join a group with the ongoing support of someone that she trusted and who was also trusted by the group. During the next three years Bianca came to enjoy the games, drawing, music, and rhythm of the group experience. For her, catechesis became synonymous with the friendship she had experienced.

At the beginning when the group assembled, Bianca would go into a corner and turn her back on everyone. She would hide when the group ate or would eat after the group left. But she loved the activities of the group, the slides and pictures that helped her understand that "Jesus is with us." She had made such good progress that her parents suggested that she be prepared for first Communion with her special friend Freddy.

The group took six months to prepare the Eucharistic celebration. They created all the symbols, giving attention to preparing the table. Invitations were addressed to all the friends who had shared in other festivities of the group. Freddy was particularly happy inviting everyone and talking about his celebration. Bianca seemed to share his joy.

Everything was ready for the Eucharistic celebration. But not Bianca. She refused to eat even though it was clear that she understood in some way that the Eucharist was more than eating food. There was no fuss. Bianca just said no. Her parents were shocked and discouraged. So were the catechists. Even when they held a quiet liturgy for the small group she had grown to trust, she still refused. Bianca spoke affectionately to the adults present; she was obviously happy to be part of the group but she would not open her mouth for the bread.

Unlike those who find their identity in self-possession, the disabled choose to find life in relationships because they know that it is only in being open to others and receiving from them that we can live. From the perspective of the Joseph Meehans of the world, neediness is intrinsic to our nature. Thus the anomaly resides not with the needy, but with those deathly afraid of saying "I am incomplete."

To be able to rest in our neediness and find power in our helplessness is key to becoming whole. We do not secure any healthy sense of what it is to be human through the arrogance of self-sufficiency, but through the honesty which confesses that to be is to need. Such a perspective turns everything around, making the people we wish to exclude "normal" and everyone offended by their openness "strange." Persons with disabilities are gifts in our midst because they teach us how we should live if we are to discover the grace of being human. Befriending them may bring a crisis of identity for us, but it is a redemptive crisis.

Jesus: Living Through the Power of God

Jesus, as exemplar of humanity and primary sacrament, was willing to acknowledge his absolute dependence on God. If Jesus was perfectly human because his whole life represented best how we should live, integral to his perfection was the ability to rest in his neediness and find power in his incompleteness. It was, in fact, knowledge of this necessity that accounted for his extraordinary openness to God. Jesus lived not in himself, but by virtue of the life he constantly received from God. McGill calls this his "ecstatic identity" (McGill 1987, 70): at every moment of his life Jesus lived not from his own power but from the power of God. What made Jesus unique was his ability to acknowledge his need, and that, in turn, opened him to the fullness of life God wants for all of us. Jesus lived "not by virtue of anything that [was] his own," but "by virtue of what the Father continually communicate[d] to him" (McGill 1987, 70). Jesus had power by resting in his neediness; it was the opening through which God entered his life and was the secret of his perfection.

What made Jesus unique was that he never saw his life as his own possession or his existence as self-achievement; rather, as McGill writes, he knew "the constituting activity of God as the constant and ongoing condition of his own being. Jesus never [had] his own being; he [was] continually receiving it. . . . He [was] only as one who [kept] receiving himself from God" (McGill 1987, 50). Jesus challenged our normal sense of existence. He showed us that we have life the same way he did: not by ourselves but through the agency of God. Our identity can be ecstatic too when we live not in virtue of ourselves but only in virtue of the life we are willing to receive. Like Jesus, we can live through the constant communication of God's love. As McGill says, "My 'I am' necessarily and constantly includes God's activity of constituting me" (McGill 1987, 51).

Seeing Jesus as the norm of all things human reverses our sense of being human. Our neediness is not something about which to be ashamed, but the door through which God's love enters our lives. Our dependence is not a weakness, but a prerequisite for fullness of life; indeed, the truth of our nature is our absolute need to receive. To the extent we are able to acknowledge our need, we receive the life which blesses us far more than we ever could ourselves. To be ashamed of our need is thus to be needlessly deprived.

Is this not, for example, the meaning of the Eucharist? The Eucharist invites us into the life-giving love of God. As a community of faith, we gather in Eucharist not because we are able-bodied and self-sufficient, but precisely because we are flawed, indigent, and frail people who hunger for the bread of life God so richly provides.

Furthermore, the Eucharist testifies that if the most basic fact of our existence is our radical indigence, it is equally true that God's response to our neediness is never-ending, life-giving love. This is the "new identity" of which the gospels speak: finding life not in self-possession, resistance, anxiety, or hardness of heart, but in gratitude for the love God longs to give. To move from anxiety and fear to openness and trust is to suffer the change of heart necessary to share God's life. "The love that passes understanding is available to us in the very act of our being, because we are constantly receiving that from our God" (McGill 1987, 52), but only those able to rest in their neediness know this.

We need persons with physical and mental disabilities in our midst, and certainly in our worship, in order to remember who we are. In their willingness to confess their dependence on others—and indeed their dependence on God—they are sacraments for us: outward signs of a more genuine humanity. God speaks to us through them, calling our attention to a more truthful way of being. We find deep truths about ourselves in unexpected places. Perhaps the most important truth disabled persons teach us is that from our neediness we receive abundant life. We need them at our side when we worship, not out of kindness to them, but as a graced reminder of why we die without the bread of life. In befriending them we embrace the truth about ourselves to which redemption responds: there is a need in us only God's love can fulfill.

The Great Undertaking of the God with a Tender Heart

In *Under the Eye of the Clock*, Joseph Meehan comments that "great undertakings require great tender rescuers with great tender hearts" (Nolan 1987, 23). He is talking about going to school with the able-bodied, and the "tender rescuers with great tender hearts" are the teachers and students who befriend him. But this is also a way of understanding what God does for us in Christ. Here the great undertaking is the redemption of the world and the tender rescuer with the tender heart is God whose tenderness comes to us through Christ, the Spirit, the sacraments, and the goodness of others.

Ethical reflections on the sacraments should not begin with explanations of what they mean or who should receive them, but with a recognition of what God does for us in Christ. In other words, we do not define the sacraments, God does. It is only by first pondering what God undertakes and accomplishes through Christ, the primary sacrament, that we rightly know what the other sacraments mean and how we are to respond to them. God's saving activity in Christ defines the substance of the sacraments; therefore, questions about who should receive them are answered not through our own sense of appropriateness but by discerning the overriding intention of God. The question is not whom do we invite to fellowship with Christ, but who is God seeking and what is God striving to achieve.

The sacraments, as manifestations of the saving presence of Christ, seek the full liberation of God in every aspect of our lives. As Mark Francis observes, each sacrament provides the possibility of bringing God wholly to life in us by uniting us with the life, death, and resurrection of Christ. As mediations of the paschal mystery, the sacraments work for the full flowering of God's redemptive love in our hearts and in our world. It is through them that the great undertaking of redemption takes place. Thus, as Mary Therese Harrington suggests, the core of the sacraments is not our sense of what we need, but God's relentless desire to offer us friendship and life. From this perspective, no one in the Church should be denied access to God's gift of salvation.

It is especially in Jesus that we understand the great undertaking of the God of tender heart. God comes to us in Christ to offer us not just a better life, but God's own life. Through the incarnation our life is not enhanced, it is transfigured, for in this offer of friendship with Christ we are invited to enter the life of God. In Christ and the Spirit we are made new creations. To transform us through love is God's mission in the world, and through the sacraments God continues the divine ministry of freeing us from death and filling us with life. The sacraments exist for the same reason that the incarnation occurred: God desires access to our hearts and to our world. Each of the sacraments testifies that we matter to God, and that God will not rest until each one of us has access to the love that saves.

In justice we are owed access to God because God desires to be accessible to us. The sacraments articulate how much God wants to be part of our lives. God wants not only to give us life, God wants to know us in the special friendship of charity, working on our behalf, seeking our good, being completely devoted to what is best for us. Christ, the primary sacrament, and all the other sacraments testify to this. They eloquently depict the personal, passionate love God has for each of us.

They capture the extremes to which God goes to be part of our lives. The gospel fact is that God loves everybody. People who love us want to be with us, and it is no different for God. The heart of God's saving ministry in Christ and the Spirit is to seek communion with humanity. This is God's abiding intention revealed in Christ and it is to this that the life and energy of God are primarily devoted. God is forever at work to establish friendship and communion with us and among us. That God lives to love us is manifest in the sacraments; and the principal duty of the Church is to facilitate, not frustrate, God's intention.

Redemption: An Act of Love, a Gift of Absolute Need

To appreciate the great undertaking of God we must remember our need for redemption. The "great tender rescuer" is God and God's act of rescuing continues through the sacraments. God reaches out to us because we need to be saved. From God's side it is an act of love, but from our side it is a gift which we absolutely need. As much as God wants to share in our life, we die if we do not share in God's. We stand in need of a rescue because we cannot ransom ourselves. As Dietrich Bonhoeffer reminds us, in ourselves we are destitute and dead. "Help must come from the outside, and it has come and comes daily and anew in the Word of Jesus Christ, bringing redemption, righteousness, innocence, and blessedness" (Bonhoeffer 1954, 22).

One of the reasons persons with disabilities may make us uncomfortable is that they remind us that we are stricken too. Living after the Fall, all of us are misbegotten creatures who "flew into the incorrect night" (DeRosa 1980, 8). We share a common affliction: wayward and misguided, wounded by the contradictions lodged in our hearts. It is our kinship in sin that makes us needy, our solidarity in corruption that leaves us begging for a rescue we can only receive. The earth is a place for the fallen and a home for the flawed. Its citizens are all those disabled by weakness and incompletion, debilitated by a disease of the spirit Christians call sin. We carry the marks of the infirm, walking about in weakness and need too glaring to be concealed. We feel currents of disorder in our hearts, forces of corruption which leave us ensnared in behavior that brings more sadness than joy. As sacraments of neediness, persons with disabilities remind us that all of us are flawed and imperfect, needing to be rescued, healed, and brought to perfect life by perfect love.

Gathered about the altar we are a communion of sinners more than saints. Looking about we glimpse our fellowship with the fallen. Here all people are one. Here all pretense of righteousness is stripped away as we who have been initiated into our own frailty extend our hands to the God who saves. At that moment we see ourselves as we are, none of us healthy, none of us whole. Our eyes are opened to the disability all share. Through sin we have been lured off center and need to be restored. Sin constitutes a disordering of all dimensions of our nature, leaving us infirm and feeble, needing to be fortified by grace. If Joseph Meehan suffered with rebellious muscles, all of us suffer with rebellious hearts. We need to be calmed, blessed, shriven, and redeemed.

The Sacraments: Lifelines to God's Love

The sacraments, as expressions of God's great undertaking in Christ, are acts of rescue and manifestations of God's relentless desire to have access to our lives. It is through the sacraments that God reaches us in our need and delivers us from our exile. Stranded in sin and needing deliverance, we wait in hope for some lifeline to God's love. As symbols of our sharing in the paschal mystery, the sacraments are lifelines to the love that saves.

Questions about accessibility to the sacraments have no meaning unless we remember the priority of God's desire to be accessible to us in baptism, forgiveness, and bread and wine. The startling and crucial point in questions of sacramental access is not that we can approach God, but rather that God humbly approaches us. Though the aim of the sacraments is to rescue us by making us new, the first transfiguration belongs to God; indeed, in the Eucharist the God of the universe rests in the hands of sinners. As Joseph Meehan reflects after receiving Communion, "Communion too brought his comforter within his grasp. . . . Communion served grand purpose, serving to bring God to him and him to servile God" (Nolan 1987, 59).

Our comforter is always within our grasp. Each of the sacraments serves the grand purpose of bringing our rescuer within reach. They underscore the shocking vulnerability of God. Ours is not a God tucked safely away in the heavens, unmolested by the terrors of life, but a God who surrenders so completely to our needs as to be held in our hands and fed to our hearts. The vulnerability of God is so extreme that through the sacraments we can take advantage of God, which is precisely what God wants. God is utterly accessible in bread and wine and every other sacramental symbol because God wants us to take advantage of the love that redeems. What is almost blasphemous about the sacraments is that they make God so easy to approach. Through them God is exposed and handed over. Collectively, the image of God communicated through the sacraments is that of a love of endless ingenuity that will do whatever is necessary to be with us. The sacraments remind us that the omnipresence of God is the incarnate accessibility of God.

The Eucharist is the point of God's greatest vulnerability, the sacrament in which God is delivered into hands that can caress or crush. But it is exactly this absolute accessibility of God which demonstrates how much God wants us to take to heart a love that saves. Scobie, a character in Graham Greene's novel *The Heart of the Matter*, captures this insight:

> It seemed to him for a moment cruelly unfair of God to have exposed himself in this way, a man, a wafer of bread, first in the Palestinian villages and now here in the hot port, there, everywhere, allowing man to have his will of Him. Christ had told the rich young man to sell all and follow Him, but that was an easy rational step compared with this that God had taken, to put Himself at the mercy of men who hardly knew the meaning of the word. How desperately God must love, he thought with shame (Greene 1971, 213).

The unflinching accessibility God expressed in such tenderness and vulnerability may also mean that God—like all of us who are God's images—is not an utterly independent being who remains unmoved and unchanging, but a God of supreme relationality who not only finds life in loving us, but is also changed by that love. This is another reason persons with disabilities are sacraments for us. In them we see God, not because they are necessarily holy, but because like them God is not afraid to confess neediness, dependence, and a great desire to be loved. To be with them is to acquire access to God, because they communicate so beautifully that God does not claim self-sufficiency and is not ashamed to acknowledge the desire and need to be loved. They witness a facet of God we often forget: God's love saves us, but our love gives God life.

> Quite simply, the challenge of learning to know, to be with, and care for the retarded is nothing less than learning to know, be with, and love God. God's face is the face of the retarded; God's body is the body of the retarded; God's being is that of the retarded. For the God we Christians must learn to worship is not a god of self-sufficient power, a god who in self-possession needs no one; rather ours is a God who needs a people, who needs a son. Absoluteness of being or power is not a work of the God we have come to know through the cross of Christ (Hauerwas 1986, 178).

The Church as Sacrament: A Community Gathered in Christ

There is a scene in *Under the Eye of the Clock* in which Joseph Meehan, in a moment of great discouragement and fear, looks to the cross and says, ''God, would you be afraid if you were me?'' (Nolan 1987, 49). The answer to Joseph's question may depend on the kind of community Christians are willing to be. We have suggested throughout this chapter that God would not fear entering the crippled body of Joseph Meehan because God already has. If the Joseph Meehans of the world are sacraments of God's presence, God is always there with them, but perhaps they need the love and acceptance of other Christians to know this.

If such is the case, who should we be for one another? Standing together, the most obvious truth about us is not that some are disabled and others are not, but that we share a kinship in need and a kinship in Christ. Our identity comes not through the strength of our muscles or the sharpness of our minds, but in Christ who brings us together. The Church is a community of those gathered not by choice but by grace. We are there only because God has summoned us in Christ. As John Huels says, all of us, whether strong or feeble, healthy or weak, ought to enjoy absolute equality in this community of faith because each of us has entered through the summoning grace of Christ.

If we are a community formed from a common calling, this means we belong to one another and are accountable to one another. We have been given one another by Christ to witness the love and justice of Christ and be faithful to the ways of Christ. God has entrusted all of us to each other, and thus we owe one another nothing less than the love and forgiveness God has given us. But the crucial fact is that God's choice of us precedes and must govern our choice of one another. It is God acting through Christ who constitutes the community of faith, and it is God's action which must shape and determine our own; in short, whoever is acceptable to God must certainly be acceptable to us. As Bonhoeffer observes, "We have one another only through Christ, but through Christ we do have one another, wholly, and for all eternity" (Bonhoeffer 1954, 26).

If this is true, certain things follow. If God's action determines membership in the Church, denying persons with physical or mental disabilities access to this community and its sacraments contravenes what God desires. This is behind Bonhoeffer's comment that "every Christian community must realize that not only do the weak need the strong, but also that the strong cannot exist without the weak. The elimination of the weak is the death of fellowship" (Bonhoeffer 1954, 94).

The strong cannot exist without the weak, nor the weak without the strong, because in a fellowship constituted not by human selectiveness but by the graciousness of God, every person is indispensable. The strength and vitality of the community is not in its members, but in the love that has gathered them. To exclude anyone is to act against the strategies of divine love by making our whim more important than God's will.

With the Church it is all or nothing. Either we accept all those God chooses to belong or we become something other than God's Church. Either we are the community of all those ransomed by Christ, or we are a community of our own choosing: a fraternal organization perhaps, but hardly the people of God. "In a Christian community everything depends upon whether each individual is an indispensable link in a chain. Only when even the smallest link is securely interlocked is the chain unbreakable" (Bonhoeffer 1954, 94).

The Church is faithful to the love of God when it realizes everyone is indispensable to God, and thus should be indispensable to us. We must train ourselves to behold one another as God does. Is this how we see one another? Is this how we behold persons with disabilities? In order to see anyone as God sees them, we must free ourselves of the idolatry which holds that anyone lovely must be just like us. Our tendency is to deem acceptable whoever is fashioned in our image instead of the image of God. We use our sense of well-being, our sense of health, even our sense of beauty to determine who should belong. But that is sinful. "God does not will that I should fashion the other person according to the image that seems good to me, that is, in my own image. . . . rather in his very freedom from me God made this person in His image. I can never know beforehand how God's image should appear in others. That image always manifests a completely new and unique form that comes solely from God's free and sovereign creation" (Bonhoeffer 1954, 93).

Thus, everyone who lives is an image of the loveliness of God, someone beautiful to God, someone to be prized and cherished. It is not for us to determine how one made in God's image should be; rather, in gratitude and joy we accept all people as beautiful reflections of God whose very existence gives glory to God. In justice we are obliged to see everyone as sacraments of God's presence, manifestations of God's life. As Bonhoeffer says, "To me the sight may seem strange, even ungodly," but God creates everyone in the divine image (Bonhoeffer 1954, 93); if this is true, to reject anyone as unworthy is to make the same decision about God.

Conclusion

Carl, the Christmas morning child who took everyone by surprise, is a wonderful, beautiful gift. And he is a sacrament—a revelation of God and a revelation of ourselves. What we have learned in pondering the mystery of this gift is that we cannot begin to discuss the question of access to the sacraments for persons with developmental disabilities until we first see clearly what it is persons with disabilities teach us about ourselves and about God. As sacraments of ourselves, they challenge us to rest in our neediness and find power in our helplessness; as sacraments of God, they remind us that the most startling anomaly is not the disabled in our midst, but the love of a God who surpasses everything we would expect. We answer questions about accessibility not when we determine who is healthy and who is not, but when we reflect on God's absolute accessibility.

That tiny child enmeshed in tubes and tape was someone to revere and a cause for awe. What we see now, however, is that what startles us about Carl's existence is not his disability, but the character of the God who lives in him. Ultimately, we learn how to treat the disabled justly when we realize that no one deviates more from our sense of the normal than God, and this is precisely our hope.

NOTES

1. In referring to persons with developmental disabilities as "sacraments," I am not speaking of the official sacraments of the Church, but indicating how persons with disabilities can reveal something crucial to our understanding of God and our understanding of ourselves that we often overlook. To speak of the developmentally disabled as "sacraments" in this sense in no way denies their need for the redemptive grace of God that comes to us through the sacraments of the Church.

2. I am grateful to Richard B. Steele for this point and for many other helpful suggestions for this chapter.

REFERENCES

Bonhoeffer, Dietrich. *Life Together.* Trans. John W. Doberstein. San Francisco: Harper and Row, 1964.

DeRosa, Tina. *Paper Fish.* Chicago: The Wine Press, 1980.

Greene, Graham. *The Heart of the Matter.* New York: Penguin Books, 1971.

Hauerwas, Stanley. *Truthfulness and Tragedy.* Notre Dame: University of Notre Dame Press, 1977.

_____. *Suffering Presence.* Notre Dame: University of Notre Dame Press, 1986.

McGill, Arthur C. *Suffering: A Test of Theological Method.* Philadelphia: The Westminster Press, 1982.

_____. *Death and Life: An American Theology.* Philadelphia: Fortress Press, 1987.

Nolan, Christopher. *Under the Eye of the Clock.* New York: Dell Publishing, 1987.

Peck, M. Scott. *A Bed by the Window.* New York: Bantam Books, 1990.

FURTHER READING

Hauerwas, Stanley. *Suffering Presence.* Notre Dame: University of Notre Dame Press, 1986. This is a collection of essays, some of which focus on a theological interpretation of suffering, the moral challenge of persons with developmental disabilities, and a Christian's attitude to the disabled.

McGill, Arthur C. *Death and Life: An American Theology.* Philadelphia: Fortress, 1987. This is a challenging and insightful book which examines the dominant understanding of the person in American society in light of an alternative Christian understanding and critique. It is provocative, beautifully written, and often very moving.

Nolan, Christopher. *Under the Eye of the Clock.* New York: Dell, 1987. This brilliant and beautiful autobiographical novel explores the experience of being disabled. There is no better book for capturing not only the challenges which beset persons with developmental disabilities, but also how the world of the able-bodied looks at them.

4

Celebrating the Sacraments with Those with Developmental Disabilities

Sacramental/Liturgical Reflections

Mark R. Francis, C.S.V.

Introduction

Many of the stories presented in this volume poignantly describe the plight of individuals with developmental disabilities being tragically refused the sacramental ministry of the Church. In quite a few of these cases one might be tempted to lay the blame for this tragedy squarely at the feet of priests who seem to be misapplying the ecclesiastical norms regulating the conferral of the sacraments. But in fairness to many of these pastors, their refusal to celebrate a sacrament (or any other liturgical rite) with a person with developmental disabilities might very well be a sincere pastoral judgement based on a particular theological conception of the nature and purpose of the sacraments. In order to understand this conception, it is helpful to look at the sacramental theology that prevailed in the Church prior to the Second Vatican Council and compare this perspective to the radically different theological approach adopted by the council in speaking about these principal liturgical celebrations of the Church. This shift in sacramental theology, reflected in the documents of Vatican

II and the revised liturgical books, is often not sufficiently understood by many who still consciously or unconsciously work out of what could be termed a "manualist-scholastic" sacramental model which tends to isolate the sacraments from human experience. The following pages will describe this changed perspective as it is reflected in the sacramental/liturgical theology proposed by Vatican II; a perspective which happily provides a more adequate theological foundation for sacramental ministry, not only with those with developmental disabilities, but with all of God's people.

The reform of the liturgy as well as the renewal in sacramental theology set in motion by Vatican II can be characterized by the recovery of two elements crucial to Christian worship that had been obscured since the Middle Ages. The first was the rediscovery of the Scriptures as an integral part of the worship of the Church and a necessary part of every sacramental celebration. The second, which particularly interests us in this essay, was the reappraisal of the symbolic dimension of all liturgical worship and the way sacraments as symbols are understood to express and celebrate the presence of God in human life. This perspective understands these actions of the Church as symbolic events that communicate God's presence within the life of a worshiping assembly and is especially important for all those involved in liturgical ministry and catechesis. Significantly, this new perspective also makes use of insights from both modern philosophy and the social sciences that describe how human beings use symbols to communicate and perpetuate deeply held beliefs and values.

This understanding of sacraments as communal, ritual symbols that mediate an encounter between Christ and the Church serves as a fruitful point of departure for speaking about questions of sacramental access for those who, because of certain developmental disabilities, have serious difficulty in approaching the world in the predominantly conceptual way long favored by our culture. Rather than regarding their reception of the sacraments as a pastoral anomaly, sacramental ministry with persons with developmental disabilities can serve to remind those of us often blinded by the excessive rationalism cultivated by our educational training that the signs and symbols used by generations of our ancestors in faith are the most expressive media for conveying what we as Christians wish to affirm about our relationship with God, with the world, and with one another because of Jesus Christ.

Sacraments and "Manual" Scholasticism

The theological approach that prevailed in the Western Church for centuries prior to the Second Vatican Council developed during the High Middle Ages (the twelfth and thirteenth centuries) and is known as Scholasticism. It bears this name because it describes a way of doing theology favored by teachers in the newly founded universities or "schools" such as Oxford, Paris, and Bologna. Their way of theologizing was greatly influenced by the rediscovery of the works of the Greek philosopher Aristotle (d. 322 B.C.E.), whose approach to knowing emphasized direct observation of the world in contrast to the idealism of his teacher, Plato (d. 347 B.C.E.). In his famous fresco in the Vatican entitled "The School of Athens," the Renaissance painter Raphael (d. 1520) aptly portrayed the starting points for both philosophical approaches in the respective gestures of Plato and Aristotle. Plato is depicted as pointing up into the heavens, indicating that his starting point is the "universal ideas" that he believed gave form to the material world. Aristotle, on the other hand, is shown gesturing downward, indicating that his starting point is rooted squarely on the earth and in the direct observation of the world, by which one can move from the particular to the universal.

The rediscovery of Aristotle at the beginning of the twelfth century not only created a revolution in the way Western theologians looked at the sacraments, but pointed the other academic disciplines in new directions as well. It was *the* scientific method of the day, and led to what many scholars term a renaissance of learning and culture during the twelfth and thirteenth centuries. While initially greeted with suspicion by Church authorities, the Scholastic theological approach was largely canonized by subsequent Church councils, notably the Council of Florence in the fifteenth century and the Council of Trent in the sixteenth century.

YOU HAVE TO SAY WHAT YOU DID WRONG

Jeff is a ten-year-old boy who is mentally retarded and cannot speak. He is a very loving boy and non-verbally responsive to what happens in the special education group. While preparing Jeff for first Communion, the pastor insisted that his parents come with him for the liturgy of reconciliation because he cannot speak or read or write. The parents were asked to tell the pastor things that Jeff had done wrong, and then the pastor gave Jeff absolution.

Although Scholasticism was presented in seminaries after the Council of Trent as the official theology of the Church, the original works of the great scholastics such as Thomas Aquinas (d. 1274), Bonaventure (d. 1274), and Albert the Great (d. 1280) upon which this theology was based were not read by seminarians. Instead, "manuals" or handbooks were used that both simplified and schematized the thought of these theological giants. Unfortunately, in an attempt to simplify complex theological explanations, it was inevitable that important nuances of the original writings were often lost. This is especially true of the way in which these manuals presented the sacraments. It is instructive to sketch just a few aspects of manualist sacramental theology since it exercised a profound influence on the theological understanding of generations of priests educated before Vatican II.

The Sacraments as Objects of "Scientific" Investigation

One of the characteristics of manualist Scholastic sacramental theology was to regard the sacraments as quasi-scientific objects of study—much like the elements of the natural universe. The manuals wished to be as specific and clear as possible in explaining the nature of a sacrament and its effects. This was due to the intense medieval concern about how sacraments caused the grace they signified—a parallel to direct observation of the natural world as a basis for philosophy. Because of this approach, however, the sacraments were often discussed in isolation from their context—the liturgy of the Church. This approach was surprisingly long-lived, and even coexisted with the discoveries of modern science. As late as the 1950s and early 1960s, for example, a debate went on among scholars in Pontifical Roman universities concerning the appropriateness of using modern physics to support the claim of a physical change in the bread and wine at the Eucharist asserted by the doctrine of transubstantiation. Electron microscopes, specialized scales, and other scientific instruments were used to try to measure the difference in a host before and after consecration. Clearly, in the minds of some of these manualist theologians, objective truth was of only one order. The sacraments, like the forces of nature and elements of the natural world, should be governed by the same laws.

This way of inquiring into the nature and function of sacraments tended to situate the sacraments outside of the context of the liturgy and to focus attention on the physical elements used in the rite rather than on the sacramental/liturgical action itself. Regarding the sacraments in this way understandably raised "scientific" questions about them which took them farther and farther away from their liturgical context. Questions such as: "Who made it? where did it come from? what causes it to be as it is? when does it cease being a sacrament? who may use it and for what purpose?" express some of the principal sacramental concerns of the Scholastic theologians. To treat these questions apart from the human and liturgical context was seen as being consistent with the concept of the unitary "objective" truth of both the natural and supernatural worlds.

Sacraments as Instrumental Causes of Grace

In light of what has been said about medieval sacramental concerns, the classic definition of a sacrament in the *Baltimore Catechism* (which was based on the *Catechism of the Council of Trent*) highlights the issue of sacramental purpose and function (i.e., what is a sacrament for? and, how does it do what it is supposed to do?). Those of us trained before the Council remember the definition well: "sacraments are outward signs, instituted by Christ, to give grace." This is still a good definition of a sacrament, but, as with any shorthand way of referring to a complex reality, all of the concepts contained in this definition need to be kept in balance; otherwise serious misunderstandings can arise.

Although the *Baltimore Catechism* refers to the fact that sacraments are outward signs, the emphasis in preaching and teaching was usually placed on the "give grace" part of this definition. Medieval theology as well as the manualist tradition affirmed that a sacrament, celebrated in accordance with what the Church intends, infallibly confers grace. This was known as the doctrine of *ex opere operato*—"from the rite performed." An individual infallibly receives the grace offered in the sacrament provided that no obstacle is placed in the way of its reception, such as serious sin or utter lack of faith. This part of the teaching was referred to as *ex opere operantis*, "from the work of the doer."

Another question then logically arose in the minds of the scientifically oriented medieval theologians: What is the minimum necessary to celebrate a sacrament efficaciously? The answer to this question was found in a close analysis of the sacrament in light of the science of the day, which divided every sacrament into its two irreducible components: "matter" and "form." "Matter" refers to the material element used in the sacrament—water in baptism, oil in confirmation and extreme unction (anointing of the sick), bread and wine in the Eucharist. "Form" refers to those words and actions deemed absolutely necessary in order to "confect" or successfully celebrate the sacrament. Over the course of the centuries, the minimum matter and form for each sacrament was determined by theologians and stipulated in Church law. For example, the minimum form for the sacrament of the Eucharist is the pronouncing of the words "This is my body, this is my blood" by a legitimate minister over the matter of unleavened wheat bread and grape wine (interestingly, the present Code of Canon Law still works with these categories). This originally hypothetical speculation contributed to a dramatic reduction in the amount of matter usually used in the celebration of most sacraments. If three drops of water on the forehead is sufficient matter to celebrate the sacrament of baptism, why bother using more? If a dab of oil from a cotton ball is enough to confer confirmation, why use a lavish amount?

Scholastic/Manualist Sacramental Theology: Positives and Negatives

The synthesis in sacramental theology proposed by the Scholastics harmonized the best of what western Europeans knew about the physical world with the Church's experience of faith in Jesus Christ. Scholasticism's identification of the septenary or seven principal sacramental rites helped to focus the attention of both theologians and the faithful on the chief ways in which Christ, through the instrumentality of the Church, continues his saving work in the world. The Scholastics made it clear that the rites confer grace only because Christ wills it, and that there must be a response in faith of the recipient to obtain the grace offered in the sacrament. These teachings emphasize the fact that sacraments are not simply words and gestures that somehow magically produce grace. They are public actions of the Church that are only efficacious because they are willed by Christ; and the grace they offer is always available because Christ is faithful to his promises.

While there were advantages in looking at sacraments in this manner, there were also definite disadvantages. These disadvantages became even more apparent when the subtle arguments of the original Scholastic theologians were reduced to easily memorized but simplistic propositions in the textbooks of manual theology used by seminaries. Some of the presuppositions about the natural world and humanity's place in it which forms the basis for the Scholastic view of sacraments also came to be questioned in light of the developments in both the natural and human sciences which began in the eighteenth century.

One of the principal problems with Scholastic sacramental theology was the relationship it presupposed (or did not presuppose) between Christ, the Church, and the liturgy (Fink 1991, 1108). While Christ was linked to the sacraments through his institution of the rite, the Scholastics increasingly began to emphasize that it was the power of Christ, mediated by the actions of the priest performing the rite as the Church intends, which objectively brings about the sacrament. This was a definite change in emphasis when compared to the earlier approach used by the Fathers of the Church. Patristic theologians attempted to maintain a balance between Christ's presence in the assembled community and the role of the priest in bringing about the Eucharistic presence. Augustine, for example, in speaking about the Eucharist, borrowed the metaphor of the body of Christ from Paul and urged believers to contemplate this great mystery by taking seriously the identification of the assembly itself with the Eucharistic species as the body of Christ. "So then if you are the body of Christ and his members it is the mystery of yourselves that is placed on the Lord's table; it is the mystery of yourselves that you receive. It is to what you are that you make the response 'Amen,' and in making that response you give your personal assent" (*Sermo* 272).

This famous affirmation of Christ's presence in the assembly was undervalued in manualist theology. Given the objectification of the Eucharistic elements during the Middle Ages with the corresponding focus on the priest acting *in persona Christi* (in the person of Christ), without reference to Christ's presence in the gathered assembly or the Word of God, the ecclesiological underpinnings for the sacraments as actions of Christ's body—head and members—were obscured. The liturgy as an action of the assembly was not seen as the privileged or even necessary place where sacraments are celebrated. The priest's presence, rather than that of a Christian community, became the only crucial factor in the celebration of the Eucharist as well as the other sacraments. In this theological atmosphere, it is easy to see why the communal dimensions of the sacramental celebration were usually overlooked by most of the manuals. Also, the traditional understanding of the role of the Holy Spirit as the dynamic force at work in any act of worship uniting the worshipers with God and with one another was usually given very short shrift or ignored in the manuals' treatment of the sacraments. Finally, because of its inattention to the liturgy as the context for sacramental worship, and a characteristic Scholastic juxtaposition of the symbol and the idea of something "real," manuals dealt very little, if at all, with the notion of sign or "symbol" as a way of understanding the sacraments—especially how symbols function within the liturgical event to express and convey the grace promised by Christ in the sacrament.

The Manualist Requirement for Sacramental Reception

One of the consequences of the Scholastic/manualist lack of attention to the question of sign and symbol was the need for those receiving the sacraments to know what the sacramental gestures and elements meant to communicate, since in their truncated form their meaning was far from readily apparent. Need for explanation was also crucial because the sacraments were celebrated in a language unintelligible to most of the faithful, and even the prayers that accompanied the sacramental gestures were unable to interpret what the rite was supposed to be about for those who did not know Latin. For this reason, much of the catechesis on the sacraments was propositional, that is, composed of descriptive sentences which summarized the nature of sacraments in general and then described the distinguishing features of each one. The sacramental catechesis contained in the *Baltimore Catechism* is a very good example of this approach. Succinct phrases describing a sacrament's function and its matter and form help the individual situate this particular rite within the sacramental economy of the Church. The statements in the *Catechism* are clear, easily memorized, but abstract. Understandably, they deal very little with one's relationship to the larger Christian community or to the sacramental event, nor do they describe the role of the liturgical assembly as an essential element in the celebration of a sacrament. Rather, discussions are usually limited to outlining the action of the one who performs the rite (the priest) and the spiritual effects of the sacrament on the recipient.

Given the highly conceptual lens through which the manualist tradition saw the meaning of the sacraments, it is logical that access to the sacraments would be limited to those who could master the concepts that explained the purpose of the rite. The rite itself, reduced by an attitude of minimalism to essential components of matter and form, was very unexpressive of the ministry and presence of Christ it was supposed to celebrate. A conceptual "understanding" of the theological propositions, then, became the all-important preparation for the reception of the sacraments after baptism. It is not surprising, then, that it was increasingly accepted during this era that the appropriate age for receiving a sacrament was linked to the age of seven—the age at which the individual was thought to somehow attain the use of reason or discretion. This is also one of the reasons why, during much of the period after the Council of Trent and until the encyclical *Quam singulari* of Pope Pius X (1910), the reception of the sacraments of confirmation, penance, and first Communion were increasingly delayed until late childhood and adolescence, or even permanently postponed for those unable to "understand."

Vatican II, Sacraments, and the Paschal Mystery

The liturgical reforms mandated by Vatican II sought to make the relationships between Christ, the Church, and the sacraments more explicit—relationships that had been blurred over the centuries because of an undue preoccupation with the sacramental "objects." Much of what the Constitution on the Sacred Liturgy and the other conciliar documents say about these relationships was inspired by a new approach toward liturgy that developed in the decades prior to the council. Theologians such as Odo Casel (d. 1948), Edward Schillebeeckx (b. 1914), and Karl Rahner (d. 1984) prepared the ground for a reappraisal of sacramental theology that took into account the way the liturgy was experienced by those gathered for worship. They emphasized that sacramental worship, far from being simply the occasion of ordained ministers consecrating static objects that "contain grace," is rather a dynamic encounter that both describes and prescribes the believer's relationship with the Risen Christ—both as an individual and as a member of the larger Church.

All of the sacraments derive their power and efficacy from the saving work of Jesus Christ summed up by the expression "paschal mystery." It is by virtue of Christ's life—his incarnation, ministry, suffering, death, resurrection, and sending of the Holy Spirit—that our faith and the sacraments based on that faith make any sense at all. It is because of the paschal mystery that Christ's presence continues today in the world—in the Church, which is his body, and in the Church's celebration of the various sacraments. This idea, of course, is not new. It is expressed in the writings of many of the great theologians, including Scholastics like Thomas Aquinas. But in the manualist tradition, this truth was often obscured because of an overconcern with the "scientific question"—what was considered absolutely necessary to confect validly a sacrament. For this reason, the Constitution on the Sacred Liturgy reminds those charged with the liturgy of the Church that for this worship to "possess its full effectiveness . . . something more is required than the mere observance of the laws governing valid and lawful celebration" (11). This "something more" alludes to how we as a community, worshiping in the Roman Catholic tradition, experience the presence of Christ in our midst.

In order to become sensitive to how the liturgy and sacraments invite us to encounter that presence we need to see the intrinsic relationship between the paschal mystery and our own lives of faith. It is the very purpose of liturgical symbols to make that link apparent. Moreover, the changed social and religious conditions of our society have made it increasingly important that we attend to the way in which our liturgical celebrations establish that link. One of the overarching goals of the liturgical reform of Vatican II was to reestablish the connection between our daily life in faith and the liturgical celebration of that life in the sacraments. Our Christian sacramental/liturgical language is ultimately not based on propositional theology or concepts about God, but on everyday human actions that our tradition has determined are sacramental because they are potentially revelatory of the intimate and loving relationship established with us by God in Christ. Everyday actions such as gathering for a common purpose with other people, sharing a simple meal, washing one another, speaking words of forgiveness and embracing each other, and massaging one another with oil are ways in which God's love and presence are expressed (Keifer 1982, 94–115). Because our culture is no longer necessarily supportive of the Christian world-view that gave rise to these ritual acts, a catechetical approach that employs abstract propositions about the effects of the sacraments will be ineffective, especially if the way in which the sacrament is celebrated does not clearly evoke the everyday human action upon which the sacramental action is based. The approach to sacraments and liturgy proposed by Vatican II invites us to turn once again to the rich, evocative, and traditional language of the sacraments—the language of symbol—in order that our worship may speak convincingly of the power of the paschal mystery. To use Karl Rahner's expression, the new theological perspective, emphasizing symbol, enables us to see more clearly the link between ''the liturgy of the world''—our life as we experience it—and the Church's liturgy (Skelley 1991, 85–105).

Sacramental Access?

The principal requirement, then, for sacramental access is that one should be able to relate to the symbolic language of the sacrament in such a way as to permit the encounter with Christ celebrated by the rite. Interestingly, a Scholastic axiom expresses this truth very well: *sacramenta significando efficiunt gratiam*—sacraments bring about grace by signifying. Traditionally, manualist theology spent much time and effort speaking about the grace part of this equation, and attended very little to the way in which the sacraments communicate God's grace. Because of this, there is a tendency for those who are working out of a propositional manualist catechetical model to be extremely uneasy in granting sacramental access to someone who cannot articulate the propositions regarding the sacrament. In confusing some of the specific meanings attached to these rites with the whole of what "is meant" by the sacramental symbol, those working out of a manualist tradition often overlooked the fact that one "knows" about the world in ways other than the strictly cognitive or conceptual. This approach inadvertently impoverishes the rich, multidimensional communication of a sacrament by reducing it to one or two verbal propositions, and oversimplifies the ways in which human beings come to know about the world, others, and themselves.

In fact, "knowing" about the world—making sense of one's identity and relationships—is often best expressed in symbols. Faith itself can be considered a kind of active knowing: an acknowledgment of a relationship with God that informs how we look at the world and others. In much the same way as Cardinal Newman distinguished "notional assent" (intellectual affirmation of concepts) from "real assent" (commitment of heart and mind to the conviction of God's love and care) (Newman 1913, 36–41), so religious educators such as James Fowler and Thomas Groome maintain that faith is better described as a verb than a noun (Fowler 1976, 175). To say that someone has faith, according to Fowler, is to assert that someone has a specific way of relating to the world and others, and of interpreting his or her experience in light of a relationship with God. This perspective on faith is a way of "leaning

A TENSE BISHOP IN A CONTEXTUALIZED LITURGY

Four special education groups had been meeting for some time in a small parish in a large city before it became clear that no one in any of those groups had been confirmed. The pastor and parents agreed on a date in May one year later when they would request the presence of the bishop for the sacrament of confirmation. The catechesis that was developed focused on the oil and the person of the bishop as the concrete symbols of the event. Even the severely retarded seemed to grasp a simple connection between Jesus and peace.

As the plans for the liturgy developed, the pastor of the parish made several unsuccessful efforts to contact the office of the bishop in order to clarify some special, simplifying aspects of the liturgy that has been planned. A request was made that the bishop come early to meet the members of the group. He was encouraged to proceed slowly with the process of confirming so that each candidate could approach with his or her family with a minimum of confusion when their names were called.

Each group met for one hour before the liturgy began to take time to be happy together, to get settled down and focused. Because there had been so much planning and preparation and anticipation of the day, the level of excitement was very high. One of the groups had baked the bread for the Communion. Other groups had been responsible for flowers and preparing the table and organizing the party following the liturgy.

The bishop arrived just in time for the celebration. He seemed uncomfortable with the people who had gathered and impatient with the pace of the service. His homily was addressed to the parents and encouraged them to bear the cross God gave them with such children. During the confirmation itself, he seemed pressed for time and therefore created a minor traffic problem by trying to hurry things along.

The bishop rejected the presentation of the bread baked by one of the groups and sent the just-ordained master of ceremonies to the sacristy for a large white host. The bishop communicated by taking the white host and then sat down. The various priests involved in the program gave Communion to the disabled. The bishop instructed the priests to put all the bread into their mouths even if they put their hands out to receive.

The catechists, perhaps even more than the confirmands, were distraught and angered by the actions of the bishop. The service was not what they had hoped it would be. At the end of the service, the bishop went to the social hall and posed for a picture with each family. The refreshment time was filled with joy and laughter and occasional spontaneous singing.

---

into life," to borrow another one of Fowler's phrases, and goes beyond simple intellectual assent to abstract truth (Groome 1980, 56–81). Christian faith is better located in the way in which we lead our lives, the choices we make day to day informed by the loving relationship God has established with us in Jesus Christ. Faith, then, goes beyond belief and involves much more than the ability to verbalize religious concepts. Real affirmations of the faith are lived responses to the conviction of this loving relationship.

As both John Huels and Mary Therese Harrington point out, while those with developmental disabilities might have difficulty in articulating the abstract descriptions of faith, it is well within their capacity to enter into the communal symbolic language used in the liturgy to express the depth of God's love for us. Therefore, it is in taking seriously the way symbols and sacraments communicate that we can develop a solid theological and pastoral approach to sacramental access for those who have developmental disabilities. What must be determined is whether or not the individual with a disability has reached the point of being "symbolically competent," capable of entering into the mystery of God's love for us expressed in our communal symbols. To discern the appropriateness of an individual's reception of a sacrament, then, it is essential that a pastoral minister be able to discern the difference between two principal ways we humans approach reality: the rational and the symbolic.

Distinguishing Two Ways of Knowing

Studies in developmental psychology as well as the other human sciences have shed light on the way in which people come to know. Human knowledge comes about through all the ways we make sense out of our world. It is evident to most of us that we do not learn all that is important in human life in a classroom. As we grow and mature we learn about the world and our place in it by using all our faculties and senses, especially the human capacity to relate to the world and others through the use of symbols which, by their nature, involve our senses, imagination, and emotions.

Since the "Age of Reason" in the eighteenth century, however, there has been a fairly constant underappreciation of the symbolic in Western approaches to education. Beginning in the eighteenth century and increasingly during the period of industrialization, Western culture consciously began to question and even distrust "facts" that were not empirically demonstrable. The reason for this is obvious: this particular way of approaching reality is necessary for advances in both the physical sciences and in the technology supported by the sciences which has made our modern industrial society possible. The emphasis on the "scientific method" as the model or paradigm for learning has made possible the gigantic strides in agriculture, medicine, and transportation which have radically changed humanity's relationship with the physical world.

At the same time, however, there has been a corresponding devaluing of the complimentary way of approaching reality that in some way is the most natural to the human person and can be termed the artistic and symbolic. Literature, the plastic arts, music, and dance are all modes of human expression that help us speak the truth about existence and to interpret our world, but they do so in a symbolic way. While rationalism seeks to dissect and analyze, the symbolic way of knowing attempts to synthesize and hold seemingly paradoxical aspects of human existence in a healthy tension. A symbol, to be a symbol, cannot be satisfactorily reduced to one meaning or definition, and might indeed evoke contradictions that point us to a profound reflection on existence which would be impossible to put into words. Ultimate questions concerning good and evil, hope and despair, life and death, are more appropriately expressed through symbol than in expository prose or speech. This is the truth upon which our liturgy and sacramental worship is based.

Very simply, we come to knowledge in ways other than the analytic, linear, and logical. While this way of knowing is extremely important for a mathematician or a physicist, it is much less important for a writer or artist. We have seen that the Scholastic/manualist theological method set great store on a more rationally based kind of knowing and interpreted the sacraments accordingly. The shift in sacramental understanding announced by Vatican II can be described as a recovery of a real appreciation of symbol and the symbolic way of knowing which had been eclipsed in the Western consciousness since the Middle Ages.

Practical Implications

There are at least two principal pastoral implications that can be drawn from this renewed appreciation of the symbolic for our sacramental ministry with those with developmental disabilities. First, it is crucial for pastoral agents—priests, catechists, and all those who minister with those with developmental disabilities, as well as parents—to be aware of the fact that readiness to receive a sacrament is not exclusively dependent on one's ability to verbalize the abstract theological propositions traditionally associated with the meaning of a sacrament. Knowing how to pronounce or spell "transubstantiation," for example, does not guarantee that one knows about the real presence of Christ in the Eucharist. Rather, it is only after an experiential reflection on the human action that underlies this meaning—for example, sharing a meal in the case of the Eucharist—that the pastoral agent can discern whether or not a person with developmental disabilities is ready to celebrate the loving presence of Christ offered in the context of the Eucharistic celebration. True understanding, then, is not dependent upon verbalization or abstraction, but is possible in those who, because of their disability, might find the purely conceptual difficult. Second, it is imperative that our liturgical celebrations recover and reflect those human actions which link sacramental actions to our everyday life. Baptisms administered with drops of water on the forehead, Eucharists celebrated with small wafers and wine only for the presider, and anointings of the sick with miniscule dabs of oil from a cotton ball will never proclaim the sacramental symbols in their fullness and will be incomprehensible not only for those with disabilities, but increasingly for all those present at the celebration.

Conclusion

While it would be a terrible disservice to celebrate the sacraments with someone who is not really prepared to enter into them, our discussion of knowing suggests that human understanding entails more than the strictly logical and propositional, especially when we try to speak about an approach to life informed by faith in Christ. It is often the experience of many who work with persons with developmental disabilities that they are quite capable of knowing what the sacraments are about. Since liturgy is primarily symbolic communication, it is very possible that someone unable to put the experience of faith celebrated in a sacrament into words and logical categories might nonetheless be very well prepared for its reception, perhaps even better prepared than those of us without developmental disabilities. The wonderful success enjoyed by the ''Vivre'' catechetical method for special religious education of which Mary Therese Harrington speaks testifies to the fact that in some ways, where the sacraments are concerned, it is those of us who are without developmental disabilities who are at a disadvantage. We who have been trained to value above all else the linear, logical, and analytical in life often miss moments of grace that are readily apparent to our sisters and brothers with developmental disabilities. We who pride ourselves on our self-sufficiency and rugged individualism often fail to make the connection between the celebration of the sacraments and our own life—a connection that seems all too clear to those who see the world as a gift and who see themselves as essentially dependent on a God whose love reaches out to them through the hands of others. When we look at the sacraments from this perspective we can legitimately wonder who is more ''properly disposed'' to receive them.

REFERENCES

Fink, Peter. ''Sacramental Theology after Vatican II.'' In *The New Dictionary of Sacramental Worship*, ed. P. Fink. Collegeville: The Liturgical Press, 1991.

Fowler, James. "Stages in Faith: The Structural-Developmental Approach." In *Values and Moral Development,* ed. Thomas Hennessy. Mahwah, N.J.: Paulist Press, 1976.

Groome, Thomas. *Christian Religious Education: Sharing our Story and Vision.* San Francisco: Harper and Row, 1980.

Keifer, Ralph. *Blessed and Broken: An Exploration of the Contemporary Experience of God in Eucharistic Celebration.* Wilmington, Del: Michael Glazier, 1982.

Newman, John Henry. *An Essay in Aid of a Grammar of Assent.* London: Longmans, Green and Co., 1913.

Skelley, Michael. *The Liturgy of the World: Karl Rahner's Theology of Worship.* Collegeville: The Liturgical Press, 1991.

FURTHER READING

Fink, Peter. *Worship: Praying the Sacraments.* Washington: Pastoral Press, 1991. Peter Fink, Jesuit sacramental theologian at Weston School of Theology, offers a collection of highly readable essays which helps the reader explore the new perspective in sacramental theology and its relationship to liturgical studies since Vatican II.

Kavanagh, Aidan. *On Liturgical Theology.* New York: Pueblo, 1984. Kavanagh, one of the most noted liturgists in the United States, sketches the contours of the relationship between the Church and the world and how liturgy and sacraments both describe and prescribe that relationship.

Guzie, Tad. *The Book of Sacramental Basics.* New York: Paulist, 1981. In a concise and readable way Guzie popularizes many of the insights of major sacramental and liturgical theologians since Vatican II. An excellent place to begin sacramental studies.

Keifer, Ralph. *Blessed and Broken: An Exploration of the Contemporary Experience of God in Eucharistic Celebration.* Wilmington, Del.: Michael Glazier, 1982. In this volume, the late Ralph Keifer, in speaking about contemporary Eucharistic theology, presents some of the basic insights on sacraments and how they both flow from and nurture human life. A fine book for adult education.

Power, David. *Unsearchable Riches: The Symbolic Nature of Liturgy.* New York: Pueblo, 1984. David Power, using insights from philosophy and the social sciences, explores the nature and function of symbol in Christian worship. In so doing, he examines the fact that the present crisis of worship is essentially a crisis of symbol and describes how we can faithfully and creatively claim our liturgical tradition.

5

Canonical Rights to the Sacraments

John M. Huels, O.S.M.

When pastors or other ministers deny a sacrament to a person who has a developmental disability, they usually believe they are following the law, the canon law of the Roman Catholic Church, which appears as canons in the Code of Canon Law[1] and as introductions and rubrics in the official liturgical books. Often pastors are able to find some justification in the law for their stance, or so they think.

However, canon law, like civil law, is a complex system which requires trained experts to interpret it properly. That is why there are canon lawyers who serve the Church just as there are attorneys who are expert in the laws of the state. The best interpretation of a Church law is not always evident from an initial reading of it. For example, when a canon requires the "use of reason" for the reception of first Holy Communion, what does this mean? Does it even apply to persons with developmental disabilities? If so, does it mean that mentally retarded persons and others with kindred developmental disabilities are excluded permanently from that sacrament?

This essay treats the canonical rights of persons with developmental disabilities to the sacraments of baptism, confirmation, Eucharist, penance, and anointing of the sick, and when they die the right to Catholic funeral rites. When canon law is properly understood, when it is seen in relation to the Church's ancient traditions and reconciled with sound principles of theology and liturgy, then the conclusions for pastoral practice will become clear. All the baptized have a right to the sacraments, a fundamental, constitutional right that exists in virtue of their baptism into Christ's Church. This right cannot be restricted unless there are clear legal grounds for doing so. We will see that, indeed, there are no clear legal grounds for denying Catholics with developmental disabilities access to the liturgical rites in question.

Baptism and Its Juridical Effects

Baptism is the fundamental sacrament of the Christian life. According to the Code of Canon Law, one becomes a person with legal status in the Church through baptism (can. 96). Baptism is called the "gateway" to the other sacraments; no one may validly receive any of the other sacraments without first being baptized (can. 842, §1). Through baptism people "are freed from their sins, are reborn as children of God, and configured to Christ by an indelible character" (can. 849).

Christ commanded his followers to go out to the nations, preach the good news, and baptize the people in the name of the Father, the Son, and the Holy Spirit (Matt 28:19). In response to this divine command, the Church strictly obliges parents to have their infants baptized and raised in the Catholic faith (cans. 867, §1; 226, §2; 774, §2; 835, §4; 1366).

Since ancient times the Church has baptized infants and others who lack the use of reason. By baptizing infants, the Church makes a clear statement about whom it considers to be human beings capable of being reborn as children of God through water and the Holy Spirit. This includes not only those who can take part in standard catechetical programs, or those who can personally attest to their faith in Christ, but all God's children, no matter what their age or level of physical or intellectual functioning. All human beings are invited by the Lord into the Christian community by means of water baptism "in the name of the Father and the Son and the Holy Spirit." By baptizing infants, the Christian community proclaims the radical equality of all God's children, and it asserts its desire that

A DEATH WITHOUT DIGNITY

Joan and Bernie had two daughters. Their second child was born with severe disabilities. Margaret was almost five months old before she left the hospital. She was seriously impaired and so fragile that her parents decided to postpone baptism until she was strong enough to be carried to church. When she was two years of age, Margaret died. The pastor of the parish that Joan and Bernie attended refused to conduct a wake service or a funeral liturgy. Margaret was buried from the funeral home without a wake, without a funeral, and without dignity. For a long time Joan and Bernie could not return to worship in the parish that had been such a significant part of their lives. When a new pastor arrived six years after the death of Margaret, Joan asked whether there was anything that could be done to bring the memory of Margaret's life to a dignified close.

every child of Christian parents ought to become a person in the Church, a member of that body that has Christ as its head.

Canon law requires that Catholic parents have their infants baptized, and an infant in danger of death is to be baptized without delay (can. 867). This law applies to all Catholic parents, no matter what the condition of their child. Provided the infant is alive, there is a serious, religious obligation to have him or her baptized. Parents are also bound to raise the child in the faith by means of Catholic education and the reception of the other sacraments, especially confirmation, Eucharist, and penance.

In canon law, an infant is anyone who is under seven years of age (can. 97, §2). Those who habitually lack the use of reason, although older, are considered legally incompetent (*non sui compos*) and are equated in the law with infants (can. 99). Infants and those who habitually lack the use of reason are not subject to the obligations of canon law (can. 11); however, they do not lose the rights that come from baptism.

Persons who lack the use of reason, even though they may be seven years of age or older, are not required to undergo a catechumenate before baptism, nor are they required to manifest their faith in any way. Some Christian denominations consider baptism to be a rite for those who are personally able to profess their faith in Christ. The Catholic Church, however, has always considered baptism, like all the sacraments, to be an action of the faith *community*.

Baptism is an *ecclesial* act. It is an incorporation of a new member into the body of Christ. This incorporation is not dependent upon a person's ability to make a personal profession of faith in Christ. Rather, it is fundamentally God's grace-filled action working through the Church community itself which makes the newly baptized one of its own, a fellow member of Christ's body. The baptized person is initiated into a community of faith. Through baptism the faith of the whole Church is expressed, concretized in the faith of the parents or guardians, the godparents, the minister, and the entire local community. The community assures that its members—whether infants or adults, whether persons with normal development or persons with disabilities—will be brought up in the faith of the whole Church and fully associated with its life in accord with each person's own condition.

Two canons of the Code of Canon Law, canons 96 and 204, speak of the important ecclesial effects of baptism. Canon 96, the first canon in the section on physical persons, states: ''By baptism one is incorporated in the Church of Christ and is constituted a person in it with the duties and rights which are proper to Christians, in keeping with their condition, to the extent that they are in ecclesiastical communion and unless a legitimately issued sanction stands in the way.'' Canon 204 appears at the beginning of the section on the rights of the Christian faithful: ''The Christian faithful (*christifideles*) are those who, inasmuch as they have been incorporated in Christ through baptism, have been constituted as the people of God; for this reason, since they have become sharers in Christ's priestly, prophetic and royal office in their own manner, they are called to exercise the mission which God has entrusted to the Church to fulfill in the world, in accord with the condition proper to each one.''

Since canons 96 and 204 are foundational for understanding every baptized member's rights and duties, it will be helpful to examine the key phrases in the two canons. This will show that baptized persons with developmental disabilities have the same rights in the Church as do all other baptized persons, each according to their ecclesial status and their own condition.

The first key phrase of canon 96 says that by baptism one *is incorporated in the Church of Christ*. The same phrase appears in canon 204. This means that the newly baptized for the first time becomes a member of the Church, a member of the body that has Christ as head.

A second key phrase in canon 96 is that, through baptism, one *is constituted a person* in the Church. This is juridical language. Canon law recognizes the personality of those who are baptized. Those who are not baptized are outside the domain of canon law. While canon law is binding only on Catholics (can. 11), even baptized non-Catholics are affected by canon law in certain respects, and they are afforded some of the rights of Catholics. For example, they can receive some of the sacraments from Catholic ministers under certain conditions (cans. 844, §§ 3, 4), or be granted Catholic funeral rites in certain circumstances (can. 1183, §3).

Canon 204 uses theological language for describing a person in the Church. It speaks of baptized persons as *christifideles*, which means "Christ's faithful" or, as translated above, "the Christian faithful." Baptized persons with developmental disabilites are members of Christ's faithful and, according to the law of the Church, are radically equal to all the other baptized. Canon 208, the first canon in the section on the obligations and rights of the Christian faithful, speaks of the equality and dignity of all the baptized: "In virtue of their rebirth in Christ there exists among all the Christian faithful a true equality with regard to dignity and activity whereby all cooperate in the building up of the Body of Christ in accord with each one's own condition and function." Again in this canon we see that baptism—referred to here as one's "rebirth in Christ"—is the sacrament which assures the radical dignity and equality of all members of the Church, including members who have various kinds of disabilities.

A third key phrase in canon 96 is that through baptism a member of Christ's faithful enjoys all the *duties and rights which are proper to Christians in keeping with their condition*. Canon 204 says that by baptism members of the faithful "have become sharers in Christ's priestly, prophetic and royal office in their own manner," and "they are called to exercise the mission which God has entrusted to the Church to fulfill in the world, in accord with the condition proper to each one." Although each canon uses a different kind of language, one juridical and the other theological, both are essentially saying the same thing: through baptism persons acquire all their duties and rights as Christians, and these duties and rights are exercised in accord with each person's own condition (mental, physical, age, status). These rights and duties include a share in the priestly, prophetic, and royal office of Christ. All the baptized have the right and the duty, in accord with their own condition, of sharing in the mission of the Church through the three "offices" by which this mission is exercised: through participation in the Church's life of worship, prayer, and charity (priestly office); through evangelization, preaching, catechesis, good example (prophetic office); and through participation in the governance of the Church, which includes many kinds of pastoral and leadership functions (royal office).

The Code of Canon Law contains a list of the basic rights and obligations of all the faithful (clergy, religious, laity) and a special list of rights and obligations for the laity (cans. 208–223, 224–231). Persons with developmental disabilities are understood to be included in all these canons, *in keeping with their condition.* The extent of active participation by the baptized in the life of the Church is determined by their own condition. The participation of persons with a severe handicap is necessarily more limited in certain respects than that of others. Nevertheless, at the most fundamental level—both theologically and juridically—all the baptized are equal and all begin from the same starting point in terms of access to their rights. That starting point is Christian baptism.

All the faithful enjoy their legal rights in the Church in keeping with their ecclesial condition and status. One of the fundamental rights of Christians is the right to the Word of God and the sacraments. ''The Christian faithful have the right to receive assistance from the sacred pastors [ordained ministers in pastoral offices] out of the spiritual goods of the Church, especially the Word of God and the sacraments'' (can. 213). Since all the faithful have the right to hear God's Word and to participate fully in the sacraments in keeping with their condition and their degree of communion with the Church, it follows that the Church's ministers have an obligation to provide them with access to the Word of God and the sacraments. In this regard canon 843, §1 on the sacraments states: ''The sacred ministers cannot refuse the sacraments to those who ask for them at appropriate times, are properly disposed and are not prohibited by law from receiving them.'' Canon 762 on the Word of God states: ''Since the people of God are first brought together by the Word of the living God, which it is altogether proper to require from the mouth of priests, sacred ministers are to value greatly the task of preaching since among their principal duties is the proclaiming of the gospel of God to all.''

Rights and obligations are complementary in canon law.

The right to the Word of God and the sacraments implies an obligation on the part of someone to provide the opportunity for others to avail themselves of their right. Since all the faithful have the right to the Word of God and the sacraments, the Church's ministers, most particularly its ordained ministers who have a pastoral office, are strictly obliged by the law to teach and preach God's Word to the people in their care and to celebrate the sacraments and administer them to those who are eligible by law to receive them. This right is enjoyed by all the baptized, including persons with developmental disabilities.

A related law of the code speaks of the catechetical formation of those with "handicaps." Canon 777, 4° says that the pastor, in accord with norms established by the diocesan bishop, is to ensure "that catechetical formation also be given to those handicapped in body or mind insofar as their condition permits." This canon specifies clearly what was already implicit in canon 213. There is a canonical obligation requiring pastors to see that persons with handicaps are given religious education—that they be nourished by the Word of God through catechesis. The first three parts of canon 777 speak of the pastor's obligation to ensure adequate catechetical preparation of children and others for the celebration and reception of sacraments, notably confirmation, first Communion, and penance. Since the fourth part of the canon is devoted to those with physical and mental handicaps, it suggests that pastors also must see that part of the religious education imparted to persons with disabilities is to include catechetical preparation for the celebration and reception of the sacraments, notably confirmation, Eucharist, and penance.

Again, pastors must see that catechetical formation be given to persons with mental and physical handicaps *insofar as their condition permits.* Nearly everyone with a developmental disability, no matter how severe their condition, can indeed respond to and benefit from catechesis when an appropriate, specialized methodology is used (see Harrington below).

Confirmation

Many people incorrectly understand confirmation to be the "sacrament of Christian maturity" which completes the Christian initiation begun at baptism. In this view, confirmation should be conferred at a time when young persons can accept on their own the promises made for them in infancy by their parents and godparents. They must be "spiritually mature" and capable of an "adult commitment to Christ." The age at which all this occurs is quite arbitrarily designated according to the preference of the pastor, catechist, or bishop who establishes parish or diocesan policy.

This "maturity" theology of confirmation is widespread in pastoral and religious education circles in North America, but its popularity does not make it any less a distortion. Confirmation is the *second* sacrament of Christian life. The Church's laws and liturgical rites envision it being celebrated after baptism and before first Communion, as in the Rite of Christian Initiation of Adults. The reception of the Eucharist, not confirmation, is intended to complete Christian initiation. One is fully initiated when one makes his or her first Communion after confirmation. The delay of confirmation until after first Communion disrupts the proper sequence of sacramental initiation and diminishes the importance of the major, or principal, sacraments of baptism and Eucharist. Baptism and Eucharist are more important sacraments than confirmation, but too often catechetical and pastoral practice belie this fact with their stress on spiritual maturity and faith commitment.

The "Christian maturity" view of confirmation inevitably leads to the wrongful exclusion of persons with developmental disabilities from their right to the sacrament. The typical parish preparation programs for confirmation demand cognitive ability. Such programs are directed toward the goal of the children or adolescents acquiring knowledge of their religion in the classroom; engaging in Christian service; and understanding, accepting, and renewing the baptismal promises made for them by parents and godparents when they were infants. Persons with significant developmental disabilities seldom fit into such a catechetical program. Nor is such a program necessary or desirable as a prerequisite for confirmation.

The standard age for confirmation in the Latin Rite Church is the age of discretion, that is, about seven years of age (can. 891). In preparation for confirmation the law only requires of those who have the use of reason that they be "suitably instructed, properly disposed, and able to renew their baptismal promises" (can. 889, §2). Those who lack the use of reason are not held to any of these requirements, and Church law does not demand that persons being confirmed have the use of reason. All that is necessary is that they be baptized.

Persons with developmental disabilities who are baptized have a canonical right to receive the sacrament of confirmation whether or not they are capable of participating in any kind of catechetical program. Even profoundly retarded persons who completely lack the use of reason have the right to be confirmed, and they should be confirmed. Parents and pastors should see to it that children with developmental disabilities are confirmed at the same age as other children, which in the Latin Church is about seven years of age, just prior to their first Communion. When confirmation is delayed beyond baptism, ideally it ought to be conferred in the same ceremony as first Communion so that the connection between the sacraments of initiation and their proper sequence is observed.[2]

Although the bishop is the "ordinary" (usual) minister of confirmation (can. 882), pastors and other priests can be given the faculty from the bishop to confirm baptized Catholics in a case of necessity (can. 884, §1). At times, there may be special reasons for a pastor or another presbyter to be the minister of confirmation for persons with developmental disabilities. For example, sometimes such persons develop a special level of trust with the priest who assists in their catechesis, and they would react more positively to the ritual actions of imposition of hands and anointing on the forehead with oil if performed by a priest they trust rather than by an unknown bishop. When a baptized non-Catholic is being received into full communion with the Catholic Church, or when the Rite of Christian Initiation of Adults is being observed, the bishop's permission is not needed; the faculty to confirm is given by the law itself to pastors, parochial vicars (assistant pastors), and other priests who have offices of pastoral care (can. 883, 2°). In danger of death, a pastor or any priest has the faculty to confirm by law (can. 883, 3°).

Eucharist

Unlike those who receive baptism and confirmation, recipients of first Holy Communion are typically required to have the use of reason (cans. 913, 914). Even in danger of death, children must be "able to distinguish the body of Christ from ordinary food and to receive Communion reverently" (can. 913, §2). However, there is abundant evidence that the canonical requirement of the use of reason does not exclude persons with developmental disabilities from the reception of Holy Communion.

Initially it should be noted that the requirement of the use of reason is a matter of Church discipline. It is a changeable, human law; it is not an immutable, divine law. For the first twelve hundred years of Christian history infants received Communion at their baptism in the Western Church, and this practice still flourishes in the Eastern Churches.

Theologically, there is no reason why infants and others who lack the use of reason cannot be fully initiated in the Church by reception of Holy Communion. They become members of the Church through baptism, and baptism makes them eligible to receive the other sacraments. Indeed, theologians today are increasingly calling for a return to the ancient tradition of full infant initiation to recognize the personhood of all God's children, even those who do not enjoy the use of reason (e.g., Searle 1987). Ideally, infants ought to receive all three sacraments of initiation in the same celebration, just as do adults and children seven or older who observe the Rite of Christian Initiation of Adults. Since infants are capable of being baptized—constituting them persons in the Church—their full initiation would better recognize their full personhood and fully respect their human and Christian dignity and equality. Unfortunately, full sacramental initiation of infants is not permitted by current canon law.

Despite the legal requirement of the use of reason for reception of first Holy Communion by children, Church authorities have treated persons with developmental disabilties as an exception to the law. For example, Cardinal John Wright, when he was prefect of the Congregation for the Clergy, wrote in 1978: "As far as the profoundly handicapped are concerned there is no doubt that they belong to a special portion of the People of God, and they do need special attention on the part of parents, pastors and educators, who should ultimately decide whether the children are ready to approach the sacraments or not" (Wright 1978).

Another indication of the more flexible approach to the law for persons with developmental disabilities is seen in the *Directory for Masses with Children*. According to the directory, those who have mental and physical handicaps are not directly treated in its norms "because a broader adaptation [of Eucharistic discipline] is sometimes necessary for them." The directory then states that its norms may be applied to those with handicaps "with the necessary changes" (Congregation for Sacraments and Divine Worship 1973).

The Code of Canon Law, in canon 777, 4°, contains another indication of the Church's thinking on this issue. As noted above, this canon obliges the pastor to see that persons handicapped in mind or body be given catechetical instruction insofar as their condition permits. Although this law does not specifically state that catechesis in preparation for the sacraments is to be given, the context strongly suggests this because the preceding parts of canon 777 (nn. 1–3) deal with the preparation of all children for the sacraments. Thus the fourth part of the canon seems to be saying that children with handicaps, whether of mind or of body, also must be prepared catechetically for the sacraments. If so, it follows that they are entitled to receive these sacraments at the conclusion of their preparation.

Policies adopted by various local Churches affirm this approach. For example, the Bishops' Conference of England and Wales issued guidelines explicitly permitting reception of sacraments, including the Eucharist, by persons with developmental disabilities (see Appendix 2 below). Another example is found in the Archdiocese of Chicago, where Cardinal Joseph Bernardin enacted a policy to promote access to the sacraments of initiation and reconciliation for disabled persons. It specifically permits reception of Holy Communion by persons with developmental disabilities (see Appendix 1 below).

Clearly, the practice of the Church is not to apply the standards of canons 913 and 914 rigorously in the case of persons with developmental disabilities. A long-standing maxim in the canonical tradition holds that "favors are to be multiplied; burdens are to be restricted." The Church does not want its ministers or educators placing burdens on its baptized members that the law itself does not place. There is also a principle of canonical interpretation which states that when the free exercise of anyone's rights is in question, the law must be interpreted strictly (can. 18). The right of access to the Eucharist could be jeopardized by an incorrect interpretation and application of the requirements of canons 913 and 914 to situations beyond those envisioned by the canons. Interpreted in a strict sense, these two canons apply to children with normal development. It seems unlikely that they should be extended to persons with developmental disabilities.

Canon 913 itself lends support to this view. It says that children are to have "sufficient knowledge and careful preparation so as to understand the mystery of Christ *according to their capacity*, and can receive the Body of the Lord with faith and devotion." Children with developmental disabilities assuredly have a different capacity than other children. Consequently, they should not be held to the same standards as other children, whether for catechetical preparation, articulation of faith, or reverent reception.

It is also helpful to note that the law has a rather flexible understanding of what constitutes the "use of reason." Nowhere does the code define what the use of reason entails, nor is the term used univocally. For example, the degree of the use of reason required for first Communion would be substantially less than that required for marriage.

In the context of canon 913, the use of reason necessary for receiving the Eucharist minimally implies the ability to distinguish the body of Christ from ordinary food, and the ability to receive the body of the Lord with faith and devotion. Even if this requirement applied to persons with developmental disabilities—and it is doubtful that it does—it is possible to understand it in such a way that persons with developmental disabilities could achieve it.

It is important for parents, educators, and pastors to realize that the ability to distinguish between the body of Christ and ordinary food is not an exclusively cognitive function requiring the ability to think abstractly. The science of developmental psychology reveals that children with normal development, from about the age of three, can partake in religious experience and can intuit the religious dimension without being able to conceptualize or articulate it cognitively. Many persons with developmental disabilities, like very young children, can apprehend the sacred on a symbolic, "preconceptual" level. They perceive through the conduct of their families and others around them that special behavior is expected in church. When they pray together with their family or another caring group they have an awareness of the sacred on a primitive level and they have religious feelings. They are able to participate in a religious event while it is happening but may be unable to reflect on or abstract from that experience. They can appreciate that the Eucharistic elements are different from ordinary food, especially in the context of the Eucharistic action, yet they may be unable to express this distinction or even be aware of it apart from the worship event.

At the level of symbolic experience, the person with a developmental disability, like the child, can often apprehend the sacred nature of the Eucharist within the relational context of the supportive and loving family and community at prayer. The meaningfulness of the encounter with Christ and the Church when participating in and receiving the Eucharist is not principally dependent on abstract reasoning but on the intuitive and symbolic apprehension of the sacramental encounter within the community setting.

Any baptized person, even a newborn infant, can validly receive confirmation and Eucharist. Baptism is necessary for valid reception of the Eucharist. All the other legal requirments governing reception of the Eucharist (use of reason, catechetical instruction, reverent reception, fasting, etc.) do not affect the validity of the sacrament. These requirements can usually be met by persons with developmental disabilities if the laws are applied flexibly to them "according to their capacity."

The pastor may not be the best judge of the readiness for first Communion of a person with a developmental disability. The pastor should listen to and respect the views of parents, guardians, and those knowledgeable in the area of special religious education. If after hearing such advice he remains doubtful about the person's readiness, then he should not hesitate to administer the sacrament. As usual in pastoral practice, cases of doubt should be resolved in favor of the baptized person's fundamental right to receive the sacrament.

Penance

Those who lack the use of reason are not capable of committing a serious sin. They do not have sufficient intellectual and consensual capacity willfully to bring about the grave rupture in their relationship with God and the Church that serious sin implies. The Church requires the sacrament of penance only of those who are in serious sin (cans. 988, 960). Therefore persons who lack the use of reason are not obliged to confess.

Even so, many persons with a developmental disability are able to benefit spiritually from a confession of their venial sins. They are able to recognize when they have done wrong. They can experience a sense of shame or guilt, and they also can experience forgiveness. If they are minimally capable of acknowledging their faults, feeling some sense of contrition for them, and making satisfaction for them (such as by performing some kind of appropriate penance), they may validly receive sacramental absolution. Often persons with developmental disabilities, like persons with normal development, experience greater benefit from the communal celebration of penance, sacramental or non-sacramental. Through the communal celebration geared to their developmental level, they can be assisted in recalling their faults and acquiring a sense of contrition.

A troubling issue for some pastors in regard to the sacrament of penance and persons with developmental disabilities is the requirement of canon 914 which says that "sacramental confession" must precede first Holy Communion. Does this also apply to persons with developmental disabilities? The remarks on canon 914 in the section above on the Eucharist apply here as well. There are many indications that this canon applies only to children with normal development, not to persons with developmental disabilities. However, even if this requirement is applied to the latter, one must realize that it is not absolute but admits of exceptions, just as it admits of exceptions in the case of children with normal development. Simple logic will suffice to prove this assertion.

The essential matter of the sacrament of penance consists of contrition for sin, confession of sin, and satisfaction for sin. To receive absolution for sin presumes the commission of some sin. Without a sin there is nothing for which to be sorry, nothing to confess, nothing for which to make satisfaction, and therefore no sacrament. But to say that every child must make a sacramental confession before being eligible to receive first Communion would be tantamount to saying that the Church demands that all children commit sin! This is, of course, patently absurb and directly contrary to the wishes of the Church. The Church seeks the holiness of its members. Therefore it is obvious that canon 914 cannot be interpreted in so absolute a sense as to require every child to make a sacramental confession before first Communion.

To interpret this law correctly, one must look at the entirety of canon 914. The canon is addressed to parents and pastors, not to children. The parents and pastor are obliged to see that children are prepared for the sacrament of penance before they make their first Holy Communion, and that they have the opportunity to confess. But no one, not even children, can be forced to receive a sacrament against their wishes. That would invalidate the sacrament. Nor may they be deprived of the Eucharist merely because they do not confess. That would be an unwarranted denial of a sacrament to which they are entitled by virtue of their baptism, their membership in the Catholic Church, and their remaining in the state of grace. Those persons with a developmental disability who lack the use of rea-

IF MARY HAS A NICE DRESS

Mary is seven years old and the youngest of six children. She is mildly retarded and has been deaf since the age of two. Mary attends liturgy every Sunday with her family. Even though she is unable to express verbally what the experience means to her, it is clear from the intensity of her attention that it is very important. It is difficult for her parents to keep Mary from liturgy even when she is sick. When they asked their pastor if she could receive first Communion, his first response was to say no because he did not see a way for her to be properly instructed. He later agreed that Mary could receive Communion because, as he put it, she looked so pious and sweet every Sunday. He suggested it would be enough to get Mary a nice dress for her first Communion. Since that time, Mary has continued to receive every Sunday with the rest of her family but she has never worn her nice dress again.

son are incapable of committing mortal sin, so they necessarily are always in the state of grace.

The requirement that a child make a sacramental confession before the reception of first Communion should be understood as a general pastoral rule, not an absolute requirement. The reason for the law is so that children from an early age may be introduced to the sacrament of penance and begin to develop a penitential piety. It is a disciplinary, not a doctrinal, rule. Doctrinally, only those who have committed serious sin are normally obliged to confess before receiving Communion (can. 916). If children or persons with developmental disabilities are not in a state of serious sin, they cannot be deprived of Holy Communion merely because they choose not to confess, nor can they be refused the Eucharist if they are incapable of confessing.

Anointing of the Sick

The sacrament of anointing of the sick is intended for persons who are seriously ill, or for old people who have become notably weakened. Persons with developmental disabilities, like persons with normal development, can only be anointed in these cases. Mental retardation and similar developmental disabilities are not illnesses; they are permanent conditions of a person. It would be insulting to persons with a developmental disability to anoint them in the belief it could make them "normal."

Canon law requires the use of reason for those who wish to receive the sacrament of the anointing of the sick. However, the extent of rational capacity that is necessary is minimal. One only needs sufficient use of reason to be strengthened by the sacrament, to be comforted by it in any way. Moreover, even persons who are unconscious can be anointed if they would have wanted the sacrament when they were in control of their faculties (can. 1006).

Note that the sense of comfort will occur more readily in a communal celebration, even if it be only a small gathering of the family or other caring group whose prayerful presence will be reassuring and comforting to the person with a developmental disability who has a serious illness.

Funeral Rites

All the faithful departed, including deceased persons with developmental disabilities, can and should be given the complete funeral rites of the Church consisting of the vigil service, the funeral Mass (or liturgy of the Word), and the rite of committal. The pastor of the parish in which the departed person resided is obliged to perform the funeral rites personally or through another minister (cans. 1177; 530, 4°). Whether or not the deceased person or his or her family had been a registered member of the parish, the territorial parish is still obliged to provide the funeral rites. One belongs to a parish in canon law by residence (domicile or quasi-domicile) in the parish territory (can. 102), not by registration or participation in the parish.

The Church's funeral rites, like its sacraments, ordinarily are only given to the faithful departed who are Catholic. With the permission of the local ordinary, baptized non-Catholics may be granted Catholic funeral rites unless this would be contrary to what they would have wished and provided their own minister is unavailable (can. 1183, §3). For example, there may be persons with developmental disabilities who are baptized but not Catholic, and who do not attend any church and therefore do not have a minister to perform religious funeral rites. With the permission of the local ordinary, a Catholic minister could perform one or more of the rites for such a deceased person, unless there was evidence that they or their guardians would have opposed the use of the Catholic rites.

The general rule is that persons who are not baptized cannot be granted Catholic funeral rites. One exception to this rule is for catechumens, who have the same right to the Church's funeral rites as do Catholics (can. 1183, §1). Another exception is for deceased children whose parents intended to baptize them. With the permission of the local ordinary such children can be granted funeral rites (can. 1183, §2). This exception could also be extended to persons who lack the use of reason, even if they are not children, whose parents or guardians had intended to have them baptized.

Vindicating Rights

We have spoken repeatedly of the legal *right* of the baptized to the sacraments, to the Word of God, to funeral rites, and related ministrations of the Church. Persons with developmental disabilities who are Catholic, like all Catholic people, have a right to those sacraments and other rites of the Church which they are eligible by law to receive. If someone believes that a person with a developmental disability has been wrongfully denied access to a sacrament or other rite by the pastor or other Church authority, he or she may take recourse against that decision (see can. 221, §1).

Many dioceses in North America have boards of mediation which have been established to resolve disputes. Anyone who wants to dispute a decision made by a pastor or another authority (other than the bishop) can bring their complaint before the mediation board. If there is no diocesan mediation board, the complaint should be directed to the diocesan bishop. In the event of an unfavorable decision, further recourse to the Holy See is possible, but this is time-consuming and often unsatisfying in its results. It would be preferable simply to seek out another pastor or priest who is knowledgeable about developmental disabilities and who will either himself provide the rites requested or recommend someone who will.

Conclusion

The Church obliges Catholic parents to have their infants baptized, and this includes infants who have developmental disabilities. Baptism and the other sacraments are sacred actions of the faith community, not mere private means of grace for individuals. Through their sacramental initiation into the Church community, all the baptized attain their fundamental legal rights in the Church, including the right to the other sacraments.

The extent of the participation of the baptized in the Church is determined by their ecclesial status and their own condition. Although persons with developmental disabilities necessarily have a more limited role in the activities of the Church than other baptized may have, they are not excluded from the

Church's most fundamental activities: hearing the Word of God proclaimed and celebrating the liturgy, including the sacraments of confirmation, Eucharist, penance, anointing of the sick and, for the faithful departed, the celebration of Catholic funeral rites.

NOTES

1. The citations from the code in this essay are taken from *Code of Canon Law: Latin-English Edition* (Washington: Canon Law Society of America, 1983).

2. Canon 891 allows national conferences of bishops to establish an age other than seven for confirmation. In 1993 the National Conference of Catholic Bishops of the United States decreed that the age of confirmation is between seven and eighteen. At the time of this writing this decree has not been approved by the Apostolic See.

REFERENCES

Congregation for Sacraments and Divine Worship. *Pueros baptizatos.* 1 November 1973. *Acta Apostolicae Sedis* 66 (1974) 30–46, n. 6.

Searle, Mark, ed. *Alternative Futures for Worship.* Vol. 2: *Baptism and Confirmation.* Collegeville: The Liturgical Press, 1987.

Wright, John Cardinal. Letter. 23 November 1978. Prot. 159082/11.

FURTHER READING

The Code of Canon Law: A Text and Commentary Commissioned by the Canon Law Society of America. James A. Coriden, Thomas J. Green, and Donald E. Heintschel, eds. New York and Mahwah: Paulist, 1985. This work contains an English translation of the Code of Canon Law and canon by canon commentaries authored by leading American canonists.

Huels, John. *One Table, Many Laws: Essays on Catholic Eucharistic Practice.* Collegeville: The Liturgical Press, 1986. This volume contains several essays on the interpretation of liturgical law and various aspects of Eucharistic discipline, including one on the Eucharist and the mentally handicapped.

Kern, Walter. *Pastoral Ministry with Disabled Persons.* New York: Alba House, 1985. This is a useful, rather comprehensive treatment of pastoral and liturgical issues surrounding ministry to disabled persons written by a priest with much pastoral experience and specialized interest in this area. The appendices include official Church documents on the disabled and various select bibliographies.

6

Affectivity and Symbol in the Process of Catechesis

Mary Therese Harrington, S.H.

Catechesis comes in many shapes and sizes. Like a garment of great value, it has to fit each person. When a person has a developmental disability that entails mental limitations, the catechesis has to be carefully crafted. The fabric of catechesis is the same from generation to generation, but the the core of the Christian mystery needs to be approached in a subtle and sensitive manner with those who have developmental disabilities, whether they be children, adolescents, or adults.

The core of the good news is that the merciful love of God is manifest in Jesus. It is treasured in the people of God who live in the love of the Holy Spirit who leads all back God. This core has been approached in various ways not only from generation to generation, but from culture to culture and now with new awareness from disability to disability. I want to focus on those who have significant mental limitations. In our relationships with them, they push us to our limits. And as we struggle with those with disabilities and they struggle with us, some valuable insights can be gained. The two most valuable insights for me that have come from this mutual struggle are the role of affectivity in catechesis and the need to develop a symbolic consciousness.

Affectivity in Catechesis

Faith education is not the same as transmission of knowledge. Faith education, catechesis, involves an awakening to the mystery that we are loved by a merciful God. It is a call to relate. One authentically relates with affectivity, be it positive or negative. Affectivity is the ability to feel and to express emotions. It is different from intelligence and will, but just as fundamental to the well-being of a person.

One can consider affectivity as background to faith or as foreground in the process of "doing" faith. As *background*, affectivity makes up the faith world into which a person is invited to enter. Since the mystery of faith is the tenderness with which God gazes on us, the role of the catechist is to give witness to this tenderness. The witness is given through the gaze of the catechist. With a person who cannot speak and is slow to respond to spoken language, the call is through one's eyes. With one who refuses to look, the invitation is through a slow process of sitting side by side until a look can be exchanged, a breakthrough experienced, a relationship initiated. The catechist takes the initiative because of familiarity with the tenderness of God.

As background, affectivity includes the sounds that one chooses to make part of an ambiance. It includes the scents of flowers, of warm bread, of cocoa. It includes the light and warmth in a room. It means that everything that is impersonal, harsh, institutional (like a traditional classroom) is avoided. Affectivity includes the whole person who sets out to lead a person with a disability on the journey of faith (i.e., the catechist, the sponsor). As a catechist, one has to tune one's own affectivity as one tunes the strings of a violin before entering into the music that is catechesis. One has to situate one's own affectivity. It is not just a question of forcing oneself to be in a certain mood. Rather, it is a question of positioning oneself to be flexible, receptive, warm, open, and totally hospitable.

The awareness out of which we move in the act of catechesis is our sense of the tenderness and compassion with which God offers us friendship and salvation. In turn, we as catechists approach our friends with the tenderness and compassion that offers friendship. The source of the love with which we love our friends is the love with which God loves us. To get in touch with this mystery, we obviously need some time and space to ourselves before we meet a person for catechesis.

Above and beyond knowing the general outline of what we want to do, we want to be aware of our own feelings. Are we dry, sad, in turmoil? Are we angry, upset, cranky? If we are convinced that our friends quickly pick up our affect and that we may be a block or a blessing to them, we become adept at fine tuning ourselves, that is, we work on our ability to feel and to express emotion. For some, this fine tuning happens through listening to a favorite piece of music. Others keep clay handy, twenty minutes with clay and they are ready. Others sit still and breathe deeply in a structured bodily position. Others go for a short walk. The point of the exercise is to clear one's head and one's heart to be available on a deep level.

Affectivity as background means also a grasp of the role affect plays in the lives of those with developmental disabilities. When a person with a disability is afraid and hesitant, the intellectual functioning that they do have is impaired. When they are relaxed and peaceful, their intellectual functioning is improved. When there is an ambiance of reassurance, there is a liberation of energy.

How often a child with normal mental capacity who is insecure or in anguish is mistaken for a child with mental retardation! If this poor state continues over time, the child actually will become mentally retarded because the whole organism is blocked in its development. A child can thus become developmentally disabled. On the other hand, when a child is surrounded by adults who respect, love and cherish him or her, even if there is brain damage or slow mental development for genetic reasons, the child thrives according to whatever capacity is possible. One cheers for the child, adolescent, young adult or adult struggling to construct him- or herself with courage and hope. One offers all the support possible to shore up a fragile equilibrium.

Any developing person needs a great deal of love and reassurance to get over the hard spots of life. As youngsters with a disability become conscious of how they are different, they struggle with their self-image. They can be demanding, capricious, moody, and angry. Some can go through periods when all affectivity seems to have atrophied and they appear much more disabled than they actually are. Others break loose in a superabundance of affectivity.

Catechists who are aware of the primordial role of affectivity in themselves and in the development of the person with a disability still have to become comfortable with the role of affectivity in catechesis itself.

Affectivity is not the same as being sentimental. It does not mean that all one has to do with people with disabilities is to love or pity them. Nor is affectivity in catechesis something of which one should be afraid. One hopes that catechesis is entered into by mature adults who are aware of their own emotions and those of our friends with disabilities. Being aware is a large part of this catechesis.

Since it is impossible to enter into the catechetical act without affectivity, the question is its quality. The quality of the affectivity is determined by the quality of the relationships. Relationships are possible with a person with a disability, even if the disability is severe and profound. Unless a person is in a coma, there is some relating going on, since they have agreed to live. The art form of catechesis is to relate to the person in order to awaken their feelings, to help them to develop a friendship and then within that friendship to venture on the journey of faith development. Naturally, this is a delicate and beautiful process.

Building bonds of friendship with those who have mental limitations is an adventure. One finds oneself looking forward to moments together because they are marked by sincerity, simplicity, pleasure, and the authenticity of mutual affection. This is as it should be. One has to look forward with desire to relationships if one is to persevere in them. However, the positive aspects of a relationship may be a distant goal to be pursued by the catechist as well as the person with the disability. A phase of negative or false relating is possible. One can spot it by the lack of confidence, spontaneity, and creativity in those involved. A struggle is in process. Both the person with a disability and the catechist need room for their own struggles with the process of conversion. Just because a phase

INNOCENCE

Vincent and Joyce have one child, Francisco, who is mildly retarded. Francisco attends special classes at a nearby public school. His parents approached their parish priest to ask if Francisco might be prepared for his first confession. In their former parish, several years before, a kind teacher had tried to give Francisco a few instructions and the parish priest had permitted him to make his first Communion. The pastor of their new parish is known to be very kind. He told Vincent and Joyce that they should not worry: God knows, he assured them, that an "innocent, handicapped child" like Francisco would never do anything wrong for which he would be responsible. Confession, the pastor insisted, was not necessary for Francisco.

is hard, one does not give up the process. One struggles on in hope of a breakthrough.

In a difficult phase, or in a negative relationship, there can be unreal expectations and manipulation on both sides. One can only wait to see how the drama will unfold. Sometimes the relationship has to be cut to allow escape before there is damage done.

In an ambiguous relationship, the catechist may want to feel good about relating to a particular person with a disability. But unless this person is loved for her or his own sake, such an adventure will be tested, tried, and found wanting. There will be no opening in catechesis, no breakthrough, because affectivity is not flowing in the right direction. The faith growth of the person with a disability can be blocked by catechists whose main motive is their egocentric need to feel good about themselves.

Affectivity in catechesis is disciplined and demanding. It has tensions, conflicts, reconciliations and breakthroughs. But its purpose is to help individuals with a disability to situate themselves in relation to others and to God. It is to help them to grow, to conquer their fears and dependency. It is a chance to conquer the autonomy that they can achieve.

How does one persevere in this drama? One needs to work with a team of catechists. The team reflects on relationships with kindness and compassion. Stategies are developed; plans are shared. Feedback is respectfully given and gratefully received.

Against this backdrop, we can now consider affectivity as an element in the *foreground* in the act of catechesis. Up front, as it were, the catechist masters language. The first thing to master is to speak in the first and second person ("I"—"you"). Third person language ("it"—"they") will never have much impact on a person with significant mental disabilities. Dialogue always has to be in direct address.

Next, one frequently speaks the name of the person with feeling in one's voice. This affirms that I am speaking to you. I know you. I acknowledge you. I call you to respond. Even in a small group, one avoids using "we" until each person feels noticed, affirmed, included, valued, and cherished.

If a person seems lost or confused, I stop to speak of what I feel. I speak of what you may feel. I try to clarify some obscurity that seems to have blocked or put a lid on the flow of communications. The flow has to continue if one is to bring a person to a moment of praise or gratitude.

Catechesis is only possible with those who have significant developmental disabilities if they feel themselves to be loved. This affectivity is the gate to their comprehension of who God is for them. One works so hard on relationships because the quality of the relationship allows the other person to discover that relating to God is possible.

Within a group of six persons with developmental disabilities and their six sponsors (one sponsor for each), the catechist works to support a whole network of relationships. Our being together is meant to build church here and now among us. The ecclesial mystery of which we hope to become more aware depends for its roots on our own relationships in our own little community of faith. It is thus that the small group becomes a privileged place for personal and faith growth. There is no competition. Each one struggles to grow according to their own capacity. Amazing gestures of love and affection are offered and accepted. Signs of concern and support multiply. Help is freely given and freely received.

In this ambiance, one can proclaim the merciful love of God. Until this ambiance is achieved, it is difficult to proclaim the good news. Naturally, with this process, communities have to stay together for a period of time. Moving from grade to grade would be counterproductive. It takes time to build relationships of quality.

The good news can be communicated in an abstract, highly conceptual, and dry manner with those who have normal intellectual functioning. It may do nothing to awaken faith. If the recipients are well brought up, they will sit and take it; however, they may drop out of the scene later on. If one tries to go the abstract way with those with mental disabilities, one is simply talking to oneself. If affectivity is avoided, how can faith be transmitted?

The Holy Spirit lives in each person, no matter the extent of their disability. And so there is one at work in the heart of the person before I as a catechist ever arrive on the scene. My work is to be in touch with the Holy Spirit within myself and thus be sensitive to work on the level at which catechesis achieves it purpose; one says the word and there is a resonance, an echo in the heart of the one who responds. This is the truest description of catechesis which we have received from the early Church.

Symbolic Awareness

The structure of symbol merits some attention before reflecting on developing a symbolic awareness. Symbolic activity always involves having a kind of double vision. One is in touch at the same time with a *here and now* phenomenon and a *beyond* phenomenon. One must keep them in tension and in balance; sad things can happen if this balance is lost.

A psychological way to look at symbol is to see the two poles as an outer and inner vision. Imagine persons very much involved in their own inner world, so much so that this inner world takes up all their attention. They may hear inner voices, they may talk to themselves, they may respond primarily to inner stimuli that no one else can perceive. We see such persons as having an emotional problem. They have lost touch with their outer vision.

On the other hand, imagine persons living totally in the outer, impersonal world. They do not reflect on what is happening to them. They are not aware of what they think or what they feel. Since they are not sensitive to themselves, they may be ill at ease with others who may need attention. We see such persons as having a superficial life. They have lost touch with their inner vision.

For the person who tilts toward a totally inner world, religion is a subjective, interior mystery. But when the focus is on the surface reality, mystery can become a kind of religious magic. Well-balanced symbolic awareness allows one to keep the everyday world and its religious significance in place. This balance between what we live and its significance is the goal of educating a person in symbolic awareness.

One presumes that God is at work not only in history in its largest sense, but also in our own histories. If God is at work today, and if I am to become aware of this, I first of all have to be aware of what I live in my own life. Then, given the way in which God has acted in the past, I become aware of traces of God's action in the present, in my life.

Persons with normal intellectual functioning can learn about God's intervention in time and space and how other people have become the people of God. Persons with limited intellectual functioning cannot interpret the past. They can only interpret the present because they lack the ability to cope with historical time. Having a historical sense requires a certain level of intellectual functioning. A person who is intellectually limited may not be able to cope with numbers or time. So five days ago, five hundred days ago, five hundred years ago, or five millenia ago may have no felt meaning. One is faced then with working out a synthesis that can be grasped in a global, symbiotic way. Because it is a synthesis, it is no less true than an analysis of history. So, one talks about how God acts more than about how God has acted.

Although a person with mental limitations may lack a historical sense, most have the capacity for symbolic functioning in the sense of early childhood development (mental age of two or three years). This kind of symbolic functioning has two aspects that are helpful in faith education.

First, such persons see things, persons, and events as totally related to themselves. This kind of egocentric functioning is not a moral fault but a phase of intellectual development. Everything of importance is "mine." The tree outside the window is mine, the moon is mine, the squirrel is mine. The advantage of this mode of knowing is that God is totally for them. This is far different from persons who admit the existence of God as an impersonal force who could not possibly be interested in them. Second, such persons have a capacity to be symbolically creative. Suppose the child sees a broom. He or she does not want to manipulate it as a broom but wants to ride it as a horse. The broom has been given a new meaning beyond its first level of meaning. Once a person can cope with a surface event, person, or thing and a secondary level of meaning or significance, there is symbolic functioning that is open to faith education.

This symbolic functioning is different from the way we relate to signs. We learn signs. A stop sign has one meaning and we have to learn that meaning. There is a one-to-one correspondence between the surface reality and the signficance. With symbolic awareness, the secondary level of meaning is global and imprecise. One gradually becomes aware of something on the level of insight. With knowledge of signs, learning is objective and impersonal. With symbolic awareness, on the other hand, there is a subjective personal attraction or aversion in an encounter with something beyond the ordinary. Symbolic awareness always involves affectivity.

The structure of symbol also requires one to be sensitive to the positive and negative valences in symbolic awareness. One can slip from one to the other rapidly. Suppose one is looking at a lit candle. If one relates to it symbolically, one enters into a kind of dialogue with it. One takes time with this dialogue. Gradually, the visible, tangible candle, while still being there, awakens a memory. This awakening is spontaneous. It is just there—a kind of evocation that brings with it vague stirrings. One flashes to a pleasant fireplace and on to the memory of the house next door that burned down. One evocation is positive and the other is negative.

Very often in working symbolically with people who are limited in their development, one has to stop to allow for this interplay of positive and negative before one can freeze a frame to move on in a symbolic progression. One starts to evoke new life but has to stop to consider that someone in the group had a goldfish that died. One starts to evoke being in the light, but stops to consider the difficulty someone has with going to sleep in the dark. One tries to move into the evocation of a person who got better but first we have to consider everyone we have ever known who died!

This normal fluctuation between the positive and the negative aspects of symbol is the stuff that develops imagination. It is a glorious event when a person with limitations starts to stumble around in this creative world. When a symbolic progression is achieved, the frame is held, the evocation is steadied, and we start to focus on how we feel with new life (having escaped death), with light (after having slept in the dark), with getting better (after not having died). The person who can move through this evocation of a lived event and can name or assent to having another name their feelings is ready to respond to catechesis.

If a person lacks the ability for deductive or inductive reasoning (mental age about 12 to 14), one does not set out to *explain* the content of faith. One asserts, one proclaims, one juxtaposes aspects of our faith with aspects of everyday life. By placing everyday life and the significance of faith side by side, a new global, symbolic awareness takes place. Eventually this develops into one's own vision of faith.

For example, suppose we talk about being in the sunlight. We talk about how it feels on our faces, our arms. We leave time to hear about being hot and thirsty, getting sunburned and people getting heatstroke! Then we go back to how good it is to be in the sunlight. We talk about feeling warm and contented. We then move on to our liturgical evocation which we place alongside this first evocation from everyday life. In this session we talk about our Easter liturgy. We focus on a real, live liturgy that we have been at together on a particular day in a particular place. We all sang . . . and there was a beautiful large candle . . . .

The work thus far may have taken forty minutes. Now we can go on to the biblical evocation. We might solemnly pick up the Scriptures and read several times, ''Jesus said, I am the light of the world; anyone who follows me will not be walking in the dark but will have the light of life'' (John 8:12). There is silence—no commentary.

Then I, as the leader, would go to each person and the sponsor sitting alongside, to give a kind of blessing. I would put my hands on their heads or, depending on the session, take their hands and say something like, ''Robert, today Jesus says to you, I am your light.'' At the end of the blessing, there would be silence and finally a song that we had sung in a liturgical setting that we can sing by heart. Finally, there might be some quiet music while the symbolic progression falls into place within each person.

In this kind of catechesis, using the French *Method Vivre* (see references), the leader is not so much an instructor as a coach.

Each person has to do his or her own work. Each one grows in the process of verbal or gesture expression. Each one learns to express what they live and what it means. But they can do their own work of hermeneutics only if they are led, little by little, and given the vocabulary, the gestures, the ambiance, and the community to support their newly formed faith awareness.

In order for such a progression to take place, there are some prerequisites. Sufficient time and a well-prepared place are essential. Contrary to what some believe—that because a person has a short attention span, one should be brief and hurry—one should rather be very deliberate and well paced. I would not begin a catechesis unless I had an hour and forty-five minutes to two hours to work. Individuals will fade in and fade out. That is normal. But when one is working in a symbolic manner, one has to allow time to settle down. One has to allow time for each person to feel what we are talking about. One has to allow time for breakthroughs in relationships and insights. One has to allow time to rest in what we do.

A well-prepared place is essential. That means not only having the proper materials at hand but also having spaces and objects of beauty. One has to love a place as well as the people in it to grow symbolically.

In such a place, with time to work, one needs well-prepared catechists or sponsors who know how to relate and who know that even with the most disabled person, we will work as a team toward four goals.

First, we will work together to develop a sense of the sacred, a sense of mystery. This implies that we approach one another as sacred. We respect one another and show it in how we speak, gesture, and move. We have a room or a corner for our symbolic progression that has the Scriptures in a special place, with fresh flowers and a candle to light. We will have only beautiful music in this space. After time in such a space for faith education we can easily move to liturgical space for worship.

Reverence will not be forced because it will have become part of the person's manner of being. Silence will not be imposed because the person will have had an education in silence.

Singing will not be strained because music will be an authentic expression.

Second, we will work together to develop a sense of the people of God. We will begin by building a community of faith among ourselves. We will express our faith together. Together we will participate in the larger assembly's Eucharistic celebrations. We will set time aside to celebrate the sacrament of reconciliation and the major feasts of the year. We will go back to our small groups to relish what happened in the larger assembly and we will prepare to contribute to the larger assembly.

Third, we will work together to develop a sense of Christ. We know that when we are happy to be together, we can proclaim the presence of Jesus. In each of our sessions, we work to come to the moment when we can hear the message of Jesus. What we do to form bonds of friendship is not just to draw those with disabilities to ourselves but to lead them to the point where, letting go of our hands, they can themselves move toward God in faith.

Fourth, we will work together to develop this movement toward God in faith, hope, and love. In each of our sessions together, we want to enter into some aspect of the mystery of the triune God where the bonds of love are such that there is but one God. We build bonds of love and friendship as a witness to that mystery and as access to participation in that mystery of Trinitarian life.

We have seen that those with disabilities are quite capable of faith education, provided that there is affectivity in abundance and that there is time, space, people, and a process that can develop symbolic competence.

FURTHER READING

Raymond Brodeur and others. *La Dynamique Symbolique.* Quebec: Universite Laval, 1989. See chapter 6 for more information on the *Method Vivre.*

Bernadette Brunot. "Affectivité et relation en catechese." *Lumen Vitae* 46, no. 2, 155–63. Affectivity is an essential element of catechesis.

Ewert H. Cousins. *Bonaventure and the Coincidence of Opposites.* Chicago: Franciscan Herald Press, 1977. This text is helpful to develop a sense of the structure of symbol.

Mary Therese Harrington. *A Place For All—Mental Retardation, Catechesis and Liturgy.* Collegeville: The Liturgical Press, 1992. Presents an overview of pastoral action.

Brian Kelly and others. *Mental Handicap: Challenge to the Church.* Lancashire, England: Brothers of Charity, 1990. See chapter 11 for an orientation to the sacraments of initiation with those who have developmental disabilities.

WHEN DAN DIED

*Dan was forty-six when he died. He had lived in the same house
and attended the same parish for over twenty-six years. When
he was young, his mother had taken him to the pastor of the
parish to ask about first Communion. She was told that Dan
did not need Communion because "he would get to heaven without it." Eventually she stopped asking. Dan continued to go
to church with his mother.*

*When Dan was forty, a team of special religious educators
began to work in the parish. After three months of preparation,
Dan made his first Communion. It was a moment of great joy
for his nine brothers and sisters. Dan was very serious about
what he did at church. He had a sense of dignity and reverence
for what was going on even though it was impossible to determine his understanding of its meaning. Dan was simply glad
to be included and so was his family.*

*Although Dan had a degenerating condition which made
it difficult for him to walk, he was always eager to participate
in the monthly liturgy adapted to the pace and interests of disabled persons. In the year following his first Communion, Dan
was part of a group that was confirmed. He also participated
in group celebrations of the rite of reconciliation each Advent
and Lent.*

*Dan died suddenly of lung complications. The wake was a
very special moment for the group of adult retarded people that
had included Dan. The eighteen people who gathered were overwhelmed with grief. Each one went forward without any fuss
and prayed and kissed Dan's mother. The following morning,
the church was overflowing for the funeral liturgy.*

7

Pastoral Epilogue

Herbert Anderson

The presence of a child with developmental disabilities moves a family to discover new ways of communicating and to learn new expressions of love. Throughout this volume we have intended to say that developmentally limited individuals are a gift to all of us because they force us to broaden our understanding of human nature. But they are more than a gift. Families with such children are challenged to foster otherwise hidden emotional resources like patience, compassion, and endurance. Many families discover within themselves new capacities for care. For some families, however, what is necessary is impossible. A child with developmental disabilities may require more than the family is willing or able to give.

The focus of this book has been sacramental access. This is, however, only one of the problems that confront families with children who are developmentally disabled. As we conclude this study, it is appropriate to note some of the familial difficulties beyond sacramental access: the grief that lingers for dreams unfulfilled; the shame that is evoked by the birth of an imperfect child because it violates our "bronze dream" of life without any signs of death; the difficulty of keeping in perspective other needs in the family as a whole; and the emotional drain of constant care and attention to the disabled individual that is sometimes overwhelming for primary caregivers in a family.

We have presumed in this study that the parents of a child who is developmentally disabled have lived through their doubts about God's goodness and come out on the other side of that struggle with a renewed and deepened faith. However, the birth of a severely limited child does not automatically lead to a deeper appreciation of the mystery and wonder of God's love. Sometimes the despair and sense of alienation from God is so profound that the journey back to faith is long and arduous, if it happens at all. It is important to empathize with those for whom the journey back to faith does not happen easily. People for whom the the birth of such a child has led to unfaith are not likely to be concerned about the possibility of sacramental access.

The Birth of Loss

It is impossible for parents to anticipate the birth of a child without dreaming. We imagine how the child will look and what he or she will be able to do. We do not imagine that the child will be severely limited. On the contrary, we envision a horizon without limitations. The birth of a child is a sign of promise for the future. In that sense, the birth of a child is always an act of faith that God will fulfill the future as God has promised. Sometimes, however, the birth of a child is expected to redeem some part of the family's past. Parents hope that a child will be able to live out their unfulfilled dreams or fill out the incompleteness of their present life. The dreams that a child is expected to fulfill often come in mythic proportions.

> Before Billie was born, I was active in the League of Women Voters and head of the Altar Society at St. Victor's Church. I played bridge and golf regularly and my husband and I were at the country club often. Then Billie was born severely limited and something happened to my image. It's like some things had to die in me. Some of the myths I believed about my life were changed overnight. They had to die and I had to let them. Now I am glad but at the time I fought against it (Evelyn).

Not everyone is as adaptable as Billie's mother. Many people insist on maintaining the myth of perfection in their family. Our children, however, seldom match our dreams. Evelyn discovered what parents with sons or daughters who are developmentally disabled all know: the birth of such a child changes everything. The myths have to die. So do the dreams and expectations that parents ordinarily have for an expected child. Letting go of dreams and myths is a profound loss for which people must grieve. It is a grieving that never ends. At each milestone, parents and siblings mourn for what might have been. In that sense, the birth of a child with a developmental disability is the beginning of chronic sorrow.

The changes that families must make may eventually be understood as a gift, but initially those changes are grief-evoking losses as well. Here is how one father described his feelings about having a child with a developmental disability:

> I have grieved the loss of the magical child, the child of my hopes and dreams; and I have felt sorrow and repulsion over the real child, the child with whom I live. I suspect this grief will continue as long as my fantasies come in conflict with realities. I look forward to the day when I can allow my daughter to freely find her rightful place within the family, and when my joy can be in who and what she is, and not in who or what she could have been. Acceptance of her mental retardation will mean granting her personhood. Acceptance will mean forgiving her for not being what I wanted [Philpott 1979].

It is not easy to grieve for losses that are not connected to death. If a child dies at birth, the sadness is overwhelming. If a child is born severely handicapped, the sadness may be initially as overwhelming but there is less freedom to grieve. Those who minister with families that include people with developmental disabilities know how crucial it is to grieve for the many losses that occur when a disabled child is born. It is experienced as interpersonal loss because the infant cannot respond to our attention as we expect. It is also sometimes an intrapsychic loss, when parents feel some responsibility for an imperfect child. Parents who feel that they know how to raise children will have less confidence in their role because this child will require different responses. When ministering to families with a child who is developmentally disabled, we need to encourage them to grieve for the birth of loss. Otherwise it will be difficult to come to love what we did not expect and cherish what we cannot always understand (cf. Mitchell and Anderson, 1983, 35–52).

When the Bronze Dream Is Tarnished

In the introduction to this volume, Edward Foley evoked Arthur McGill's metaphor of the "bronze dream," which points to the widespread conviction that we should be able to live without negatives like crab grass, body odor, crooked teeth, disability of any kind, and death. Because our society is so intent on avoiding negativities in life, we are inclined to hide what we cannot accept and ignore what reminds us that we are finite. Parishes are not much different. We would rather that those with a disability worship at a "special" liturgy because sometimes they are disruptive. The enthusiasm and unpredictable spontaneity of the developmentally disabled is experienced by many families and parishes as more chaos than they can tolerate. Even when we know that they have been thoroughly prepared through catechesis, we have lingering worries about uncontrolled and unpredictable behavior.

Although we will continue to challenge Christians not to be seduced into believing that real life looks like the "bronze dream," we must be cautious about criticizing too harshly parents who have difficulty accepting the birth of a child with severe limitations. Suffering is always in the eyes of the beholder. Our expectations of life, faulty though they may be, determine what we experience as suffering. We don't need to have a mythic view of reality to expect that our children will not be limited from birth. One of the hardest pastoral tasks is to allow people to mourn as loss what others might perceive as gift.

> Sarah was small at birth. Everything else seemed normal except that Sarah was born thrusting out her tongue in an uncontrolled way. She lost some weight at the beginning but we were not alarmed. She was very quiet but we were glad not to stay up nights. Sometimes we worried because she was so weak but the doctors advised us to wait and see. We came to think of our Sarah as a "late bloomer." Our Sarah was nine months old before we learned the truth. She was

> born with Down's syndrome. She was mentally handicapped from birth. It was several weeks before I could tell people at work about my daughter. First I was ashamed and then I was ashamed because I was ashamed (Charles).

The self-esteem of a parent is often dealt a terrible blow by the birth of a child with mental retardation. The dreams for self, which are woven into the dreams for the child, are shattered by the reality of the mental limitation. If a parent's world is woven together by a fabric without seams, then the birth of an imperfect child will create shame by tearing the seamless robe. Maybe Evelyn in the story above did not go to the "country club" because she had less time. And maybe she did not go because she was ashamed. There are other times when the birth of a disabled child is perceived as punishment for sin. The shame for the child covers a hidden guilt. Whatever the reason, it is important to understand and accept the shame of a parent like Charles for the birth of a child like Sarah who did not fit his picture of a perfect daughter. Our pastoral ministry to families with members having developmental disabilities should not make it harder for such families by expecting prematurely more acceptance than is possible.

There is yet another and even more complex dimension of the birth of a child with developmental disabilities. "Although there are more than 250 known causes of mental retardation, Fetal Alcohol Syndrome constitutes the leading cause of mental retardation today" (Stark 1992, 252). Such a totally preventable cause raises a serious challenge for the Church to be engaged in advocacy for public policies that will protect the unborn from abuse *in utero*. It also changes our pastoral work with families from comfort to challenge if, in fact, the disability of a child is the result of a mother's carelessness during pregnancy. The rights of parents are less significant than the responsibility of the family to create a safe and hospitable space even before a child is born.

The Impact on the Family

The addition of any child into a family by birth or adoption changes many things. Roles shift and ritual patterns of interacting are modified to accommodate a new member in the family system. When the new child is developmentally disabled, ordinary changes are intensified. Such a child needs special services, unique learning environments, additional health care, and an alternation in routine parenting patterns. Because these demands are not likely to diminish, the affect on the family's functioning is both intense and permanent. The strain on a marriage is reduced when the parents have a common strategy in response to the needs of the child. It is not the birth of a child with a developmental disability that itself threatens the vitality of a marital relationship, but how the family as a whole responds to the special needs of the child.

The life cycle of a family is built upon the assumption that as children grow older they become increasingly autonomous. If a child is incapable of this ordinary movement, the dynamics of a family's life will be fundamentally altered. Some families limit the growth of everyone in order to stay connected to the one who is limited. Other families, however, are able to honor the uniqueness of each member and respond accordingly. What is important to note is the reciprocal influence of the members of any family system. The presence in a family of a child with a disability makes it more difficult for the system to overlook the uniqueness of any of its members.

Ordinarily, changes in the developmental competence of family members requires alternation in family rules as children grow up and grow older. Sometimes, the diagnosis of a disabling condition for one member is so upsetting that the family as a whole "freezes" at the state of organization it had at the time of the diagnosis. Other families will isolate the member with the disability so as not to impede the growth of others. The demands for change may come from outside as well as inside the family. When a person with a developmental disability becomes capable of living independently outside the family, both parents must acknowledge this increased independence and increasing competence. If one parent is dependent upon being the caregiver of his or her disabled child, it may be difficult to accept this ordinary change for a child who is extraordinary (Foster and Berger 1985).

Near the beginning of the novel *Family Pictures* by Sue Miller, Nina recalls her vision of how the family began.

This was the way it had worked, I thought: My parents had made their family, they had the requisite three pretty children, they'd bought a house on a street in Chicago where other young couples were buying houses in the years after the war. My father's career was flourishing; they loved each other.

And then it all went haywire.

Randall sat in their midst, more beautiful than the first two, but immobile. At two, he still didn't walk. He didn't speak except when whole sentences, out of context, dropped from his mouth, as though someone invisible were using him as a ventriloquist's dummy. He seemed possessed, my mother has said enchanted. Under a spell.

Sometime in the process of Randall's diagnosis—he was variably and at different times thought to be deaf, retarded, autistic, and schizophrenic—my mother got pregnant with me, as though she thought another child would break the spell. Mary followed a year later, and then Sarah a year and a half after that. From the start we knew what was expected of us. We were to be normal, happy. We were to make up for Randall's illness, Liddie's resentment, Mack's wild struggles. Sometimes, looking at us, my mother's eyes would fill with tears. "Oh, my perfect babies," she'd say, and swoop down on whoever was closest to hold her up against her broad, strong body.

For my parents, and for Lydia and Mack, deciding what Randall's illness meant and figuring out what to feel and do about it became lifelong preoccupations. Mostly it meant they struggled with each other, since they all disagreed about him. For us, though, for Mary and Sarah and me, Randall was a given. Sometimes he was in the way, but sometimes he was useful to us: he was the troll under the bridge, he was the baby in the carriage, he was the bogeyman, the prince, the father (Miller 1990, 11–12).

Sue Miller's novel portrays what is known by every family that includes a child with a developmental disability: nothing can ever be the same. When families are free to grieve the loss they feel, to acknowledge the complexity they experience, and to honor the uniqueness of each family member with relative equality, then the difference need not be a disaster but an invitation to a deeper and richer family life. It should not be assumed, however, that every family has the adaptive skills to make that possible.

When the Need for Care Does Not Diminish

For their families, those with developmental disabilities are more than "spiritual guides and friends" who point us to the necessity of God's graciousness. They are people whose care is emotionally demanding. Long after parents have lived through their grief and overcome their shame, they are faced with the unrelenting demand to care for their child. The participation of people with developmental disabilities in the worship life of the Christian community is a powerful source of support for their families. When children are excluded, so are the parents. When those with disabilities are included as full participants in the life of faith, the parents are included as well. And their inclusion is one great source of support.

The Christian community understands the importance of care as well as cure. We understand our pastoral ministry to be valid and meaningful even when no significant contribution is made to the cure of individual sickness or situational distress. For that reason we care for the chronically ill, offer companionship to the dying, sustain and encourage those with developmental disabilities, and console those who grieve when we cannot change what is wrong. The compassion of a Christian community for those who suffer is a sign that God is present even when health is absent. Even though healing is never complete, wholeness is still possible. It is a gift that comes from God through the compassion and care of others. Whole people are those who are joined to the suffering of others.

There is yet another dimension of care for the parents of those with developmental disabilities that goes beyond inclusion. Those families who keep their children at home as long as they can need support and maintenance. People with developmental disabilities are indeed a reminder to us that life is finite. For their parents, however, the awareness of finitude is sometimes overwhelming. These parents may have limited access to the outside world. They are not as free to come and go as other parents. Moreover, the strain of care while balancing the demands of other family members is both satisfying and emotionally draining. Beyond inclusion, the Christian community needs to provide support and encouragement for families whose emotional resources are being drained by the obligations of ongoing care and the agony of chronic sorrow.

These resources are diminishing even before they are drained for an increasing number of such families. They feel isolated without access to support systems. Medical costs are rising. When both parents work, there is less leisure time and less energy for ordinary responsibilities and fewer resources to care for a daughter or son within the community. More than any other volunteer institution in society, the Church is in a position to be a catalyst for supporting families, allowing them to use the natural community resources in ways that honor their individual choices as well as cultural, social, and spiritual differences (Stark 1992, 251).

Finitude and Incompleteness

Families of the developmentally disabled understand human finitude and the limits of creation in a unique way. They also know about their own limited energy in a way that makes finitude more than a theological abstraction. The Christian community is in a position to be supportive of families when they are overwhelmed because we understand finitude as part of the human condition. Families and individual parents need not be heroic. Being overwhelmed is not the same as being unloving. Parents are free to discover their own limitations within the context of a believing community that acknowledges finitude as a gift from God.

> Bobby had been brain-damaged since infancy. He loved to talk, although it was not always clear what he said. At age 52, he found his way into the church and eventually wished to be baptized. Bobby's Uncle Ben, a permanent deacon in the parish, presided at the baptism. They had rehearsed carefully that after the baptism was over, Uncle Ben would shake Bobby's hand as a sign of welcome. Ben took Bobby's hand at the conclusion of the baptism to say welcome; at that moment, Bobby said in a loud voice "Welcome Ben!" and proceeded to welcome everyone within reach.

When parents and families grow impatient because one of their children is limited from birth, they need to be reminded that the world is an unfinished place. Those with developmental disabilities are not the only ones who are unfinished, however. We all are. And it is this incompleteness that everyone struggles against. No one wants to die with dreams unfulfilled and tasks unfinished. But it is so with us all. Vulnerability and social interdependence are at the center of what it means to be human. Our inability to accept being unfinished or incomplete is one source of human suffering. The real challenge for any Christian community is to be a gathering of people who are free to struggle with being unfinished. When that happens, the Church can be a remarkable place of support for families of those with disabilities, because it is where we all struggle together in our incompleteness.

REFERENCES

Foster, Martha and Michael Berger. "Research with Families with Handicapped Children: A Multilevel systemic Perspective." In *The Handbook of Family Psychology and Therapy*, vol. 2, ed. Luciano L'Abate. Homewood, Ill.: The Dorsey Press, 1985.

Miller, Sue. *Family Pictures*. New York: Harper Collins Publishers, 1990.

Mitchell, Kenneth R. and Herbert Anderson. *All Our Losses, All Our Griefs*. Philadelphia: The Westminster Press, 1983.

Philpott, James L. "By the Waters of Babylon: The Experience of having a Down Syndrome Child." *Pastoral Psychology* 27, no. 3 (1979), 155–63.

Stark, Jack. "Presidential Address 1992: A Professional and Personal Perspective on Families." *Mental Retardation* 30, no. 5 (1992), 252.

Appendix 1

Access to the Sacraments of Initiation and Reconciliation for Developmentally Disabled Persons

Pastoral Guidelines for the Archdiocese of Chicago

1985

This seems an appropriate time to examine sacramental opportunities for developmentally disabled parishioners. While sometimes referred to as mentally retarded or brain damaged, in these guidelines they will be referred to as developmentally disabled persons.

Often they live in institutions, some in residential settings in our neighborhoods. Others remain at home with their families. Most of them would formerly have stayed close to home, but now many go to school or work and they participate in sports and recreation. Similarly, although their participation in parish life would most likely have been passive in the past, now they are to be *welcomed as full members* of the parish and, in particular, the liturgical assembly.

The Liturgical Assembly

The liturgical assembly is the gathering of all the members of the local parish who stand before the Father, offering thanksgiving and praise. This gathering is always in the process of growth—growth in faith in God and in respect for persons. One challenge to the parish is to discern and decide why and how to assimilate developmentally disabled people into its life through the sacraments.

The parish's liturgical life provides a dynamic context which can help them, regardless of age, to break out of isolation and discover others as believers. It provides an opporunity to help them overcome fear of others. It also helps each parishioner to have the courage to risk something to build solidarity, to build unity, to build up the Body of Christ.

The parochial assembly provides continuity in the sacramental life of all its members, including those who are developmentally disabled. If families cannot bring *all* their members to the parish church, where can they bring them? If each person does not have a place before the table of the Word of God and the table of the Bread of God, where is there a place?

Nevertheless, to provide an appropriate atmosphere of dignity and reverence for worship requires leadership, common sense, and a strong sense of respect for the assembly as well as for each disabled person.

The Family

The disability of an infant, child, teenager, or adult is a terrible blow to a family. The disability threatens the equilibrium of all the relationships among family members—parents, brothers and sisters, grandparents and the larger family. It also can challenge faith in God as a merciful Father. Sometimes a family needs to pull back for a time to cope with anxiety and rebuild its bonds. Often only gradually can the family approach the parish leaders to request a sacramental celebration.

To respond well to such a request, parish leaders need sensitivity and the ability to listen attentively. They are not responding merely to the disabled person but to his or her whole family.

The family has a right to expect sacramental participation and the catechesis involved for its disabled member. This is so even if progress is slow and the process is not always serene and easy. On the other hand, the parish and its leaders have the right to expect the family to be involved in the religious or faith education of its family member. In this process, in other words, there is a mutual relationship between family and parish.

For a variety of reasons, some developmentally disabled persons who live in residential settings do not have contact with their families. In these instances, the relationship between the administrators of the residence and the parish leaders becomes especially important to ensure proper pastoral care for these members of God's people.

The Developmentally Disabled Person

Developmentally disabled persons may live at home or in a residential facility. They may be able to speak or may be nonverbal. They may be able to walk or may live from a wheelchair. Nevertheless, such individuals are human beings, each with his or her own ways of relating within the world. Abstract, conceptual thought may not be possible, but there are other ways of knowing, such as symbolic or intuitive thought and/or response.

Religion is neither fundamentally abstract nor purely conceptual. It is primarily relational, and, for that reason, the developmentally disabled person can be educated in faith.

It was often said in the past that such pesrons needed only the sacrament of Baptism in order to go to heaven. However, today we see how persons—even those with severe disabilities—are transformed by belonging to a loving community of faith. We observe how the sacramental event gives people a history, a larger family, a feeling of belonging, and a future.

In the past, whether or not a person had reached "the age of reason" was generally determined by the answer to the question, "Does this person understand the sacrament?" However, today the term is understood as referring not just to knowledge, but also to autonomy. Developmentally disabled persons are often dependent on family or sponsor to initiate a sacramental event. But, just as there are many ways of knowing, so there are also many ways of expressing consent and nonconsent. This makes it essential to get to know each person well to make certain that each knows and consents to the sacramental event according to individual capacities.

The context of sacramental initiation for developmentally disabled persons is the quality of their relationships. Relationships which are inviting and welcoming, and which foster insight and assent, allow them to awaken gradually to the larger sacramental dimension of life. This active, spiritual nourishment is a far cry from the days when some parents took their children from one parish to another with the hope that someday someone would give their children Communion. No parent should have to go outside of the local ecclesial community for normal sacramental participation. The assembly which integrates developmentally disabled children into its celebrations can experience its own transformation and rejoice in the growth of all its members.

The Sponsor/The Catechist

A pastoral process is necessary to initiate any person into the parish's sacramental life. Often baptismal godparents are more honorary than functional. In the case of developmentally disabled people, the parish might consider carefully selecting some of its members to be sponsors, so that these members can be with them and help them in their sacramental initiation into the parish's life.

Disabled children, adolescents, young adults and adults may be grouped with their peers and their sponsors into small communities of faith. Local parishes may work together to build supportive bonds among these people. Attempts to give individual sacramental instruction to a developmentally disabled person will, in most instances, lead to frustration for all concerned, whereas sharing life in a group stimulates faith, hope and love.

It is disrespectful to the person and to the family to administer a sacrament before there has been adequate catechesis, but it is equally disrespectful to prolong catechesis indefinitely or to avoid celebrations in the larger assembly because of fear, embarrassment or prejudice. At some point, the catechist must make a prudential judgment and, if it is a positive one, affirm that this person is ready for the sacramental event even when the ordinary signs of this readiness may seem remote. A catechist can only make such an affirmation if he or she has taken time to build an authentic relationship with the person. A true relationship understands beyond words or sounds, communicates beyond definitions, and frees persons to be at their best beyond simple behavioral control. True catechesis takes time, but is often most effective *after* a sacramental celebration, when ever greater meaning is discovered, based on common lived experiences.

The Priest

The presider at a sacramental event, interacting with a developmentally disabled person, needs the skill and capacity to relate to others in the sacramental exchange.

When a significant disability is involved, the celebrant needs to prepare carefully for the sacramental celebration. He needs an opportunity to get to know the person and to receive honest answers to his legitimate questions. Often the catechist is the bridge between the family and the priest, assuring the family that questions do not imply rejection and assuring the priest that a person has been prepared according to his or her capacity and that requested adjustments are reasonable. (The archdiocesan agency SPRED [Special Religious Education] is a resource available to families, catechists, and priests in this process.)

During the sacramental celebration, it is most important that the priest relate effectively with the developmentally disabled person by slowing his pace, being more deliberate in gesture and speech, being gentle, and using language which communicates directly and clearly.

The priest may need to emphasize part of the readings of the day or use only part of them rather than rework the entire liturgy of the Word. He may also consider using the second of the Eucharistic Prayers for Masses with Children, which has frequent acclamations. A liturgy such as this, scheduled monthly, can accommodate people with a wide range of disabilities. This special liturgy can also have an impact on musicians, ushers, and other family members and celebrants so that beneficial adjustments influence all other liturgies in the parish. While we often expect to help developmentally disabled persons change or grow, in the process we frequently, to our surprise, find ourselves changing as well!

As time goes on, this practice may help developmentally disabled persons feel comfortable enough to participate in other liturgies. Inclusion in appropriate parish liturgies is often more important than developing ''special'' liturgies exclusively for them.

Baptism

Through Baptism a person enters into the life of Christ, the life of the Church, and, concretely, the life of the local parish. This mystery needs to be visible and tangible to all concerned.

When presenting for Baptism a developmentally disabled infant, parents are still in the throes of shock. In fear and uncertainty, and possibly in hurt and anger, they are trying to enter into a new rhythm of life. This is an important time for parish members and staff to show their care and concern for the entire family. Perhaps another family in the parish has lived through a similar event and is willing to be of assistance. With the encouragement of the parish staff, there can be some bonding between these families for mutual support.

If the disabled person is older, the usual process of the Rite of Christian Initiation of Adults is to be followed. In this instance, the director of the catechumenate and the sponsor/catechist must foresee where adjustments are needed according to the needs and capacity of the individual.

Confirmation

''In Confirmation we are more intimately joined to the Church and endowed by the Holy Spirit with special strength.'' (*Constitution on the Church*, #11).

Developmentally disabled persons, who have been baptized and have agreed to belong to a community of faith through catechesis and liturgy, are not passive members of the Church.

They are full members who belong and contribute according to their capacity. A child who is profoundly disabled and cannot speak or move can still contribute to those around him or her by a loving presence. Developmentally disabled members of the faith community belong fully to the community. Each contributes according to his or her capacity to give and our capacity to receive. Each is confirmed as a member according to his or her capacity.

When family members, facility administrators, religious workers or catechists request the sacrament of Confirmation, they are giving witness to the bonds which exist between the Church and the developmentally disabled person. They desire to express that relationship to the assembly gathered around the bishop so that the body of the Church may be built up in love. In the assembly, the bishop affirms that the disabled person is a full member of the Church, filled with the Holy Spirit—a member of the family of Jesus, offering praise and thanksgiving to the Father.

In the celebration of the sacrament of Confirmation, the person's age is to be respected. Developmentally disabled adults ordinarily should be confirmed with other adults. If they are baptized as adults or received into full communion with the Roman Catholic Church, they should normally be confirmed at the same time. In keeping with the Church's ancient tradition, the Easter Vigil is the ideal time for Christian initiation.

Eucharist

By what signs can a developmentally disabled person indicate readiness for the Eucharist? They are *desire, relationships* with people who share faith and prayer, and a *sense of the sacred* as manifested in behavior. Often these people cannot use words which express their understanding of the difference between ordinary bread and the Bread of God, but they can show that they recognize the difference by their manner, the expression in their eyes, their gestures, or the quality of their silence. God's desire to be in communion with the person can be presumed; the person's desire for communion must be awakened and sustained.

When developmentally disabled persons are in the assembly and feel bonds with those around them, it is normal for them to have a desire to go to Communion. Families and catechists should foster that desire, nourish it, and arrange for the first Communion while the desire is alive. A precise catechesis elaborating the meaning of the event in greater detail is often more fruitful *after* first Communion.

Sometimes a person is so disabled that it is difficult for him or her to approach the minister of Communion. Then it is appropriate for Communion to be brought to the person in the pew.

Sometimes a developmentally disabled person is too ill to go to church. A liturgy in the home or residential facility is then the most appropriate occasion and place for first Communion.

When a developmentally disabled person is dying, providing Viaticum should be considered.

Reconciliation

The sacrament of Reconciliation can be very fruitful in the lives of developmentally disabled persons. Often they have had the experience of being offended by others or of offending others without knowing exactly how this alienation happened. Participation in a celebration of Reconciliation can help them sense a new beginning in these relationships.

Such persons frequently are comfortable in parish celebrations of Reconciliation, especially during Advent and Lent. When they approach the priest, if they have poor communication skills, a question which elicits a "yes" or a "no" can be very effective.

Sometimes several communities of faith—composed of developmentally disabled persons, their families and their sponsors—may gather together for a special celebration of the sacrament of Reconciliation. The process of going to the priest may be difficult for those who have problems walking, and communication may be difficult because of communication disorders. In this setting the liturgy can be adapted to the communication and relational gifts and limitations of those present. In this way, gathered together, they can effectively celebrate the merciful love of the Lord for all God's children.

Catholic Burial

As a full member of the Church, a developmentally disabled person has the right to a Catholic burial.

When the person dies in close proximity to his or her family, the parish celebrates his or her life and witness and offers the honor due a Christian. The person is entitled to the Church's Rite of Christian Burial including the celebration of the Eucharist. Family and friends who request the Church's complete rites for a developmentally disabled person should not be denied them.

When the person dies in a residential facility, the family can make arrangements which are normal for any Catholic. If the person is a ward of the State, his or her record should show that the family or guardian requests a Catholic burial. The leaders of the local parish should welcome and claim the body for burial. We belong to one another and to God our Father. We are all members of the communion of saints.

Conclusion

By welcoming developmentally disabled people through the waters of Baptism, the oil of anointing in Confirmation, the consecrated bread and wine of the Eucharist and the peace and joy of Reconciliation, the parish builds up the Body of Christ.

''From our parents and grandparents we have received the rites by which we give thanks, intercede, anoint and confirm, marry and bury. We do them over and over, and we teach our children to do them. Thus do we discover what it is to be a Christian and a Catholic. We learn this in hearing the Word of God, in the hymns and acclamations, in the genuflections and the kneeling, in the greeting of peace, in sharing the consecrated bread and wine at the holy table. The liturgy is not an 'extra,' something nice that may give us good feelings. It is our life, our very spirit. It is the source of our identity and renewal as a Church.'' (*Our Communion, Our Peace, Our Promise*, pastoral letter on the liturgy by Joseph Cardinal Bernardin, Chicago, 1984).

Appendix 2

"All People Together"

A Statement of the Roman Catholic Bishops of England and Wales

January, 1981

The Community and the Disabled Person

1. The total community has a responsibility towards the disabled members of the community. Until our own day handicapped people were hidden people. They were segregated people. They were denied the support and research which could lead to integration. Now the tide is turning.

The priority of this special year is to make everyone more aware of the aspirations, the abilities and the needs of disabled people. Disabled people must be treated as equals, integrated into the life of the church and the community. We must listen to disabled people and respond accordingly.

2. Many thousands of generous people have dedicated themselves to the severely handicapped people in residential care. Their love and patience is, for the most part, hidden from the public eye and seldom receives public acclaim. Their generous work, undertaken day and night, is a sign of Christ's charity and an extension of Christ's love. But this is also a question of justice and "the demands of justice must first of all be satisfied: That which is already due in justice is not to be offered as a gift of charity" (*Decree on the Apostolate of the Laity*, n. 8). The ideal of this year may be frustrated by debate, by economic restraint and by sheer lack of sympathy on the part of the com-

munity, but the underlying emphasis on integration and welcome is right. The Second Vatican Council insisted that "God who has fatherly concern for everyone has ruled that all men constitute one family and treat one another in the spirit of brotherhood" (*Constitution on the Church in the Modern World* n. 24).

3. But the brotherhood of the human family must be real. It is the church's task not only to change individual hearts, but also the "collective consciences of people," even to the point of "upsetting through the power of the Gospel mankind's criteria of judgement, determining values, points of interest, lines of thought, sources of inspiration and models of life" (*Evangelisation in the Modern World,* nn. 18, 19).

The Year of Disabled People is not just a review of our kindness to individual people; it is an examination of our values. These values are so often related to wealth, physical prowess or instant, but shallow attraction. Success is measured in terms of power and possessions. This whole culture downgrades the handicapped person.

All this shows itself when financial priorities are set. The Christian message is one of concern, especially for those who are the weakest. It is with dismay that we see more resources dedicated to destruction. To declare a Year to the support of disabled people and at the same time transfer resources from their support is a contradiction. We plead that the balance in the distribution of our resources be revised in favour of the disabled.

Attitudes to the Disabled Person

4. Ignorance, prejudice and even superstition concerning disabled people are difficult to dispel. We must recognise, first of all, that they are people before we apply to them the term "disabled." This is a comprehensive term. It includes sensory handicaps such as blindness or deafness. It includes physical handicaps which restrict mobility, bodily control or communication. It includes mental handicaps which limit normal intellectual development.

Some degree of disability is part of growing old and the disabilities of age can cause rejection. This is a bitter experience, especially for parents set aside by their own children. On the other hand, the sacrifice and generosity of adults committed to their elderly parents can become a frustration of their own lives and even conflict with their duty towards their own family.

5. So disability is not academic. It is a very tragic feature of human life. The constant struggle of those who are parents of a handicapped child or the dismay of one who is afflicted by a permanent disability later in life can be the secret only of those personally involved.

The result of all this can be a turmoil of guilt, anger, frustration, disbelief and resentment. These are human emotions. No one must feel any sense of moral guilt when these emotions become overwhelming at a critical moment when God's love and even his very existence are challenged by the mystery of disability.

6. There are some extreme reactions to disability. There are those who wish to eliminate handicapped human beings altogether, but abortion and euthanasia are immoral and superficial solutions. This was referred to in our statement in January, 1980, on the evil of abortion.

Post natal neglect which amounts to infanticide is repugnant to any civilised society. While we are not bound to use elaborate and extraordinary methods of keeping people alive, there is the very real obligation to offer the normal supportive care which is the right of every human being. The church must be a defender of these rights of disabled people, especially by defending the right to life itself.

7. Having protected the very lives of disabled people we must also sustain their dignity and respect. Rejection must not give way to over-protection. This can be equally undignified. It reduces the potential of disabled people and frustrates the growth of those faculties which are normal. The act of caring must never become an added limitation. Extreme forms of disability will require total support. There will always be such a need. But the basic policy must be the development of any potential which may be present, the welcoming of all people

into the total community and the education of our parish and diocesan families for the policy. Jesus Christ gave us the example of reaching out to those on the fringe of the community. As the presence of Christ in the world, the church must accept the same standards and responsibilities.

The Voice of the Disabled Person

8. At the centre of our discussion is the one who is actually disabled.Think of people who are mentally handicapped. Some may seem oblivious to all the distress which is so apparent to those who love and care for them. Indeed, stress may be known only to those who attend to their needs.

9. But even with severely handicapped people communication can be established, especially by those who are attuned to the handicapped person concerned, and provided communication is not restricted to verbal communication. Handicapped people look for the complete range of communication which can match their disability. To deny them this is a real injustice and deprivation.

Handicapped people can be aware of personal limitations and the reactions which these limitations arouse in other people.

They can be conscious of rejection or know that they are a burden. Some, especially those of high intelligence and sensitivity, can analyse only too well a situation where they are not only limited themselves, but the cause of restrictions on other people—an extended disability. The family may have to be reorganised because of one disabled person who then suffers an added embarrassment.

10. In some extreme cases the handicap causes revulsion and this can be sensed by the handicapped person. Impatience may be caused by a slow reaction or a limited capacity for communicating. A corresponding frustration is built up in the disabled person. Dignity can be affronted by contrived compassion or superficial and ill-adjusted conversation, offering a highly intelligent person only the thinking attuned to a severely mentally handicapped child. The result can be loneliness and exclusion, disillusion and resentment.

Handicapped people too easily know rejection. They are made aware of their "difference." While most people are eager to establish their unique qualities, disabled people are anxious to prove that they are fully human. "Handicapped people are not looking for pity. They seek to serve the community and to enjoy their full baptismal rights as members of the church" (*Statement of the United States Catholic Conference:* November, 1978).

The Mystery of Disablement

11. Disablement is a mystery. Mysteries, although beyond our comprehension, always invite us to deepen our understanding. Thus, to speak of disability as "God's will" is misleading. God desires only that which is good.

So the presence of the handicapped person is not only a challenge to our charity and sense of justice—it is also a challenge to our faith in a loving God if people, especially innocent people, must suffer and demand so much of those who care for them.

12. In the human condition everyone is imperfect. Despite our longing to be self-sufficient we are all interdependent. We categorise people according to race, religion, age, culture or skills but the truth is that there is much more unity than division in God's creation. We share more than we possess uniquely.

Disabled people are full members of the human family. Not only do they belong to the human family but they are very much part of the paradox of the human condition. In some mysterious way we must struggle to gain the happiness for which we are destined. Each person must experience a calvary before a resurrection. A human being free of suffering is less of a human being, and in this mysterious conflict the handicapped person has a special witness to offer.

13. The disabled person is a sign who unites, brings together people to form a community in a spirit of service. How frequently people of different, even opposed, traditions and faiths will combine to meet the needs of their fellows in distress. The handicapped person can be the focal point needed

to unite and reconcile those who are, apparently, more fortunate. This "power of the handicapped" is the power to arouse care and service. The very disfigurement which may make us question the love of God, in fact arouses an active love which brings us nearer to God and to one another. Far from segregating disabled people we should recognise them as central to our human inadequacy. They can lead us on the way of the cross, a way set out not just for a few, but for every person on the way to God.

14. With this in mind how can we deny the disabled person not only a place, but a central place, in our society and in our church? It is here that the strength of Our Lord's example can reassure us. For him the prime concern was the outcast, including those who are physically or mentally limited: people in some way set aside. And yet it was he who revealed his loving Father. For him there was no contradiction. While we are not offered a solution to a mystery, we are given reassurance by the attitude of one in whom we trust and from whom we receive our inspiration.

The Disabled Person and the Sacramental Life

15. Through the sacrament of Baptism disabled persons are members of the church. As a consequence they are encouraged to share in the full sacramental life of the church if this be at all possible. Those whose task it is to administer sacraments must be eager to ensure that a physical or mental disability does not lead to a spiritual deprivation. Priests and teachers must be sensitive to the intuitive interpretations of parents and others who are close to disabled people and who can sense their mood.

The whole emphasis of the church's attitude must be one of welcome and supportive encouragement. Care must be taken to ensure that the things of God are not misused, but it is equally important to ensure that what God offers to his children is made available to them. Certainly no priest should refuse a disabled person any sacrament without making sure that he appreciates what the disability is and how it is to be interpreted.

16. Especially is this true of the mentally handicapped child. The sounds and emotions of the child may mean nothing to a stranger or to a priest inexperienced in these matters. But a parent, who is the child's first teacher, a specialist teacher, can be attuned to the child and know that appreciation, even reverence is being expressed in signs which may be unusual, but are genuine and adequate. A mentally handicapped person usually relates intensely to those immediately present—parents, brothers and sisters. This quality of relationship can develop and extend to others to whom the parents relate. A handicapped child can grow to relate to Christ because the parents explicitly do so. Intuition can bypass the usual reasoning processes and develop a prayer life and an appreciation of sacrament which is not expressed in words and can only be detected by a parent deeply in tune with one who relates in this unusual but genuine style. Pope Paul VI in his address on *The Pastoral Care of Handicapped and Maladjusted Youth* in October, 1973, said that communication includes "One's simple presence, by a look, silence or appropriate language."

17. Confirmation establishes us as witnesses to the world. The part each member of the church plays will be conditioned by the circumstances in which people live. The disabled person is giving a serious witness to the paradox of Christianity. This bitter sweet theme is essential to the Gospel message and given clear prominence by the Christian person who is disabled. This was supremely displayed by Christ himself who died that we might live and suffered that we might have happiness.

Because the disabled person can arouse the generosity of so many other people there is an involved presence in the community which should be sealed with the Sacrament of Confirmation. The ability to bring together people of many faiths, and of none, is an outstanding apostolate. The reception of the Sacrament of Confirmation by disabled people is more than a kindly gesture—it is a recognition of the active mission which is so effectively theirs.

18. Disabled people must be made welcome in the liturgical life of the church, especially at Mass where the commu-

nity of the faithful gather. Within this is the sacrament of Holy Communion—the supreme sign of unity with Christ and his church. Into this holy unity is gathered the unity of parents with their handicapped child and the unity within the family is consecrated when the family comes together to receive Our Lord in the Eucharist. Because the sacrament is so sacred it must never be diminished or reduced by mindless reception and a child of normal mental ability is expected to have an explicit faith in the real presence before receiving Holy Communion.

19. But the mentally handicapped child may be incapable of being so explicit. Such a child is already a child of God by faith and Baptism and all such are invited "To come together to praise God in the midst of his church, to take part in the sacrifice and to eat the Lord's Supper" (*Constitution on the Sacred Liturgy*, n.10). If the church is insensitive to the variety of human situations there is created a "double disability," a limitation of understanding on the part of the church which adds an unnecessary frustration to that which already exists. Approaching the time when it is the practice to receive Holy Communion, the mentally handicapped child may not be able to formulate distinctions which are usually required before admission to the sacrament.The priest whose task it is to administer the sacrament must make sure that he has used every possible means to interpret the mind of the child and, in addition, be encouraged by the faith of the family of which the child is almost certainly the center. When parents are devout and generous the community of the family supports the child in faith. We already see this in the baptism of children.

Pope Paul VI asked: "How can she (the church) contribute to the integration of the handicapped into modern society, if she does not endeavour to have them recognised as full members of her own?" (*The Pastoral Care of Handicapped and Maladjusted Youth*: October, 1973).

20. For a physically handicapped person the sacrament of Reconciliation can be distressing rather than encouraging. The physical effort of entering a confessional, the inevitable revealing of one's identity, the limitation of communication: these are examples of what can be an embarrassment and frus-

tration rather than a moment of welcome and reunion. Sorrow must be present, but in cases of extreme speech limitation this may have to be expressed other than by words. This is the traditional sensitivity for which the church has always called.

21. The person with a severe mental handicap is in need of particular understanding. While some may be too limited to understand this sacrament, by the same token it can be presumed that they are too lacking in conscious decision to be in need of the sacrament. On the other hand, a restricted experience of their condition may cause a priest to misread the situation. Parents and others who have been closely associated with the mentally handicapped testify to the sense of right and wrong which can develop. The automatic labelling of the mentally handicapped as incapable of wilful fault does not fit the facts. There is frequently an intuitive ability to understand wrong and a sorrow which can be recognised in the explicit joy which may follow forgiveness. Mentally handicapped people are not just innocent children: they may become adults and capable of guilt.

The priest may find difficulty in recognising signs which the parent can interpret very clearly. Neat expressions to describe facts are beyond the capability of many disabled people and the task of priests and of parents together may be to express for them what is already in them. Signs, gestures and facial expressions can reveal an adequate disposition for reception of this sacrament.

22. The disabled person needs to love and be loved. The disabled person needs to feel lovable. This basic need—basic to all human people created by God who himself is love—is expressed in many ways: within family life, by a generous and trusting friendship and, in a unique way, between husband and wife in marriage. For some people a mental or physical handicap will exclude the possibility of such a relationship. But this must not be presumed. On the contrary, the natural right to marry must be respected unless the person concerned is clearly either unable to understand what they are doing or unable to sustain a life-long commitment of marriage.

23. Within the group—the very large group—of people we

call disabled there are many persons who are very suited for married life. The limited research done on the stability of marriage between disabled people suggests that there is better prospect of a permanent commitment between people who marry while disabled than between people who have no apparent handicap. Because of this, support should be given to those who, although in some way disabled, show a serious desire to marry and are able to make a life-long commitment. Serious consideration would have to be given to the implication of having children and caring for them. However, we must recognise the right of handicapped persons to enter marriage and the witness they can give to the beauty of married love.

24. Because the understanding of disability has been limited and even distorted in the past, there has been a hesitancy on the part of society to allow disabled people to take an active and official role in the community. More recently there has been a positive policy of allocating essential work to such people. Initial expectations have not altogether been fulfilled, but the message is clear. The church must be prepared to accept and use to the full a disabled person who is called to the "priesthood and religious life." Certain disabilities will always exclude such a possibility and the ultimate decision must rest with the bishop. But a growing appreciation of individual potential must change attitudes. The ideal is for full integration wherever this is possible. The many ministries of the church can be enriched by the involvement of those people of God who are so obviously close to the sufferings of Christ. Especially can one who is disabled be an effective minister to one who is equally limited and in need of understanding.

25. The total attitude of the church to handicapped people must be encouraging. If they are baptised they are members of the church and those who administer the sacraments on behalf of the whole people of God must look for the best way for disabled people to enjoy full sacramental life if this be at all possible.

Integration in Practice

26. The National Pastoral Congress meeting in May, 1980, expressed deep concern for the mentally and physically handi-

capped members of the community. The Congress singled out the spiritual needs relating to the sacraments and the very practical needs such as access to buildings.

Many statements on these matters have been issued by commissions and other agencies. We add as an appendix to this message a quotation from one of these documents. We urge that during this special Year these documents be studied and acted upon in the pastoral areas of our countries. We call on church organisations to ensure that their activities are open to disabled people, that they are welcomed as full members and that, to overcome any reticence from whatever cause, a firm invitation be sent to such people to join the full apostolate.

27. The general strategy is one of integration. While people who are extremely handicapped may be housed in special accommodation, the emphasis must always be to welcome handicapped people into the community. The family is the first support, but it is unreasonable to expect the demands of handicapped people to be met by the family alone. The wider community of the neighbourhood and parish must be prepared to play its part becoming, in a new sense, an extended family. Parents who become exhausted by their own generous care of handicapped children cannot be blamed if they question the logic of those who defend the life of a handicapped child, but ignore the child's claim to a worthy place in society.

28. Bearing in mind Pope Paul's insistence that our attitude towards handicapped people is a test of our own integrity as followers of Christ, we must be involved in their education, their instruction in the faith, their participation in the liturgy and in the social life of the church. Study of their welfare should be a part of priestly formation and included in diocesan courses for clergy. Our welfare agencies should respond to their needs and the needs of their families. We must speak for and with the disabled people when their requirements can be met only by the resources of the total community.

29. We trust that those who already work with the handicapped members of the community will be encouraged by this special Year devoted to disabled persons. Many others will be encouraged to offer their support. Our response is a demand on our charity and a reminder of our duty. It is also a test of

our civilisation. The nation which cares for those who cannot care for themselves is a nation which can see beyond a superficial distortion to the deeper beauty of God's creation. Our response is a test of our faith as we recognise disabled people as children of God, our brothers and sisters in Christ.

The following is an extract from the leaflet issued by The Social Welfare Commission in 1980, entitled ''The Handicapped Person in the Church.''

Practical Suggestions for Parishes

Community Life

1. Look at your church and see whether it makes a provision:

   A—for easy access for physically-disabled people by providing ramps or handrails if necessary; and appropriate space for wheelchairs. Information about planning or adapting church premises to facilitate access can be obtained from the Centre of Environment for the Handicapped, 126 Albert Street, London, NW1 7NF. (Tel (01) 267 6111, ext. 265).

   B—for deaf people, by installing a few special pew hearing aids if required, or the Loop system. For general information regarding the use of the Loop in churches, contact: The Westminster & Brentwood Pastoral Services for the Deaf, Ephphatha House, 73 St. Charles Square, London, W10 6EJ (Tel: (01) 969 8415).
   For technical information, contact: Royal National Institute for the Deaf, 105 Gower Street, London, WC1E 6AH. (Tel. (01) 387 8033).

   C—for arranging, from time to time at least, to provide transport to Mass for people confined to the house or in residential establishments.

2. Look at your community and find out whether handicapped people are encouraged to join in any local activities—discussion groups, youth groups, clubs, or societies with special interests, whether they are attached to the Church or not.

3. Look at your neighborhood and see whether your local authority is doing all it can to make public facilities accessible to physically disabled people. This would include libraries, museums, art galleries, concert halls, theatres and evening classes (and lavatories). Link up with other churches or groups who are also concerned about this. Your local Council of Churches (where it exists) is a good group to approach to carry out this kind of survey.

Personal Life

1. Look out for families with a handicapped member and see:

> A—whether everything possible is done to help them to play a full part in parish life, and that they are being visited regularly by clergy or by parishioners, if they wish;

> B—whether they are in touch with any organisation which might help them. But do not leave it all to organisations; it is the personal touch which is important. You might sometimes find that you can be a voice for those handicapped people who cannot speak for themselves;

> C—that they get all the support and help they need if there is a crisis in the family.

2. Look out for any handicapped child or adult living near you, and see if a neighbourly helping hand is needed:

> A—to "baby sit" and allow parents to go out together sometimes, including giving them freedom to attend Mass together if the child cannot be taken to Church,

> B—to take an adult out, either to Church, to do shopping, to the library, to a theatre or concert, or just for a drive;

> C—to do shopping for an older person who is becoming increasingly disabled, to visit and chat as a friend, or to do odd jobs about the house, or to read to a blind person.

3—Welcome handicapped people into your own home and if you have children encourage them to invite a handicapped child to join in as many games as possible. Remember that some parents and handicapped adults are hesitant to ask for help, and they may need you to make the first move.

Distressing as it is to say so, it is still necessary to remind ourselves that a person with a handicap is not less a person. The failure of many non-handicapped people to treat those who are handicapped as individuals with equal value is one of their greatest difficulties.

About the Authors

Herbert Anderson is a Lutheran pastor, and professor of pastoral theology at Catholic Theological Union. The co-author of *All Our Losses, All Our Griefs,* he has written *The Family and Pastoral Care* as well as numerous articles on pastoral care and pastoral theology. He is co-authoring a five-volume series entitled *Family Living in Pastoral Perspective,* the first volume of which is entitled *Leaving Home.*

Dianne Bergant, C.S.A., is professor of Old Testament studies at Catholic Theological Union. She is the editor of the Old Testament Series of the *Collegeville Bible Commentary* and former editor of *The Bible Today.* She is working in the areas of biblical interpretation, biblical spirituality, and social issues such as ecology, feminism, justice, and peace.

Edward Foley, Capuchin, is associate professor of liturgy and music at Catholic Theological Union in Chicago. He is editor of The American Essays in Liturgy series from The Liturgical Press. Among his numerous publications are *Rites of Religious Profession, The First Ordinary of the Royal Abbey of St.-Denis, From Age to Age,* and *Foundations of Christian Music.*

Mark Francis, C.S.V., is assistant professor of liturgy at Catholic Theological Union. Co-editor of *Living No Longer for Ourselves: Liturgy and Justice in the Nineties,* he is also the author of *Liturgy in a Multi-Cultural Community* and numerous articles on liturgical adaptation and multi-cultural worship. His doctorate in liturgy is from the Pontifical Liturgical Institute of St. Anselm.

Mary Therese Harrington, S.H., is a member of the Chicago Archdiocesan Pastoral Team for Special Religious Education (SPRED). She is a practicing catechist with adolescents who have a wide range of developmental disabilities.

John M. Huels, O.S.M., is associate professor of canon law at Catholic Theological Union and major superior of the Eastern Province of Servites.

Barbara E. Reid, O.P., holds a Ph.D. in biblical studies from The Catholic University of America and teaches New Testament at Catholic Theological Union. Her scholarly interests are in the Synoptic Gospels, Paul, and feminist interpretation of Scripture. She has published in *Biblical Research, The Bible Today,* and *New Theology Review.*

Paul Wadell, C.P., is associate professor of ethics at Catholic Theological Union. He is the author of *Friendship and the Moral Life, The Primacy of Love: An Introduction to the Ethics of Thomas Aquinas,* and *Friends of God: Virtues and Gifts in Aquinas,* as well as several articles in Christian ethics and spirituality. He received his Ph.D. from the University of Notre Dame.